LET IN

LET
IN
THE
LIGHT

CENSORSHIP SECRECY AND DEMOCRACY

BRANDON

First published in 1993 by
Brandon Book Publishers Ltd.
Dingle, Co. Kerry, Ireland

British Library Cataloguing in Publication Data is available for
this book.

ISBN 0 86322 173 4

This book is published with the financial assistance of
The Arts Council/An Chomhairle Ealaíon, Ireland

Cover designed by the Graphiconies
Typeset by Brandon
Printed by Colour Books Ltd, Dublin

For all those throughout the world who are fighting the most subversive fight – for the right to be heard and the right to know.

FOREWORD

IT WAS QUITE a remarkable sight. The queue snaked up two flights of stairs, across the cavernous concourse, out of the building and down across the square. They had started gathering more than two hours before the meeting was due to begin, and even with several hundred accommodated in an overflow hall, hundreds would be turned away – and all that before they knew that Salman Rushdie was due to speak. The next day the two large halls were again filled to bursting point.

On 15 and 16 January 1993 Trinity College played host to a conference on censorship and secrecy called "Let in the Light". Its organisers, a disparate, small group of journalists, academics, lawyers and trade unionists, saw the meeting as a way of drawing together a number of issues that had until then been the focus of separate debates that never seemed to overlap.

The rows about abortion information or about Section 31 of the Broadcasting Act (which prohibits interviews with proscribed organisations), the seemingly never-ending succession of revelations about dubious business and political practices and golden circles, the threats to prosecute journalists for not revealing sources, even the banning of Madonna's silly book – all these issues, though ghettoised in debate, were, we felt, related symptoms of a closed society, of a society that didn't trust its own people to make decisions for themselves. The struggle for freedom of information in Ireland, in all its facets, is a key to the process of exposing humbug and hypocrisy and empowering citizens to create a new society, above all a society, in John Major's words, "at ease with itself". That spirit of change was aptly summed up by Albert Reynolds in an interview with a magazine shortly after he was appointed Taoiseach when he promised to "let in the light" on Irish society.

The conference struck a chord. A new government had been elected. Promises were being made about open government, reviewing censorship provisions, making public the funding of political parties. But the promises have yet to be acted upon, and the agenda set by "Let in the Light" is still a powerful indictment of Ireland in 1993 – a view substantially endorsed by the recent report of the UN Human Rights Committee.

This book is the edited proceedings of the conference. The editors have sought to preserve, as much as possible, the actual words spoken by our guest speakers, though some trimming has been necessary because of length. The unevenness of some parts of the text is thus not so much a reflection on the contributors but the result of the natural differences between spoken and written language. The views expressed are not necessarily those of the organisers, but the spirit of the whole is very much that of "Let in the Light".

Thanks are due to hundreds of people and organisations for making both the conference and this book possible. The unions NUJ and SIPTU were particularly generous, as were the two hundred individual sponsors of the conference (see appendix). RTE and *The Irish Times* gave invaluable sponsorship and assistance as did Trinity College, whose unflappable Senior Dean, Dr P.J. Drudy, was put through the hoops. The Conrad Hotel were very hospitable. Two of our speakers, Carl Bernstein and Anthony Lewis, flew in from the States; others came from Brussels, Britain, and all over the country. All the speakers' willingness to give of their time for no other reward than contributing to "the cause" is much appreciated. The M.Sc. Communications students of the Dublin Institute of Technology taped the conference.

Above all, our thanks go to Salman Rushdie, who put himself in considerable danger to travel to Ireland and participate in the conference. We hope that the visit, which included meetings with President Mary Robinson, government ministers and representatives of all the major parties, and of unions, writers and artists, will contribute to ending the outrageous *fatwa*. His visit would not have been possible without the tireless and seamless help of the Gardaí, Article 19 (the international campaign against censorship), the Abbey Theatre, the Arts Council and many others deserving of thanks who prefer anonymity.

The support of Brandon and Steve MacDonogh, himself a battler for free speech, is very much appreciated.

Ellen Hazelkorn and Patrick Smyth

"Let in the Light", now a permanent campaign against censorship and secrecy, can be contacted at 9 Brendan House, Brendan Road, Dublin 4.

Contents

Foreword   7

Secrecy and Censorship   11
Kevin Boyle   11
Carl Bernstein   17
Salman Rushdie   26

Government and Business Secrecy   39
Michael Mills   39
Anthony Lewis   40
Dr Garret FitzGerald   48
Mary Raftery   59
John Tierney   67
Susan O'Keeffe   73
Michael Mills   80

Publish and Be Banned   83
Steve MacDonogh   83
Maxine Brady   92
Damien Kiberd   101
Patrick MacEntee   109

Censorship and the Arts   121
Luke Gibbons   121
Robert Ballagh   125
Neil Belton   129
Cathleen O'Neill   137
David Collins   142

POLITICAL CENSORSHIP 147
Mary Holland 147
Alex White 149
Jake Ecclestone 156
Bill Rolston 161

**DEMOCRACY AND FREEDOM
OF INFORMATION** 169
Frances D'Souza 169
Dr Anthony Clare 173
Aidan White 177
Patrick Smyth 180

An Appeal 183
Contributors 186

SECRECY AND CENSORSHIP

Kevin Boyle

When this conference was but a twinkle in the eye, the discussion focused on the idea of a small seminar. The assumption, the false assumption, was that it would not attract enough people to fill a hall and perhaps we should hire the back room of a pub or a hotel.

We had wrongly judged the interest among Irish people, ordinary Irish people, on these issues. We had wrongly accepted the wisdom of some politicians that these questions about freedom of information in a democracy are technical matters which are really only about the press banging on about its own interests.

It is a great privilege for me to be given the opportunity to chair and open this important conference on censorship, secrecy and democracy in Ireland. It's quite a relief, in one sense, to come from London, where, of course, the other island has its own information problems, its own preoccupations with royal exposés, Calcutt and Camillagate and so forth.

Indeed, the series of exposés and battles between the government and the tabloid media bring to mind in many Irish memories the experience of the first months of 1992 when in Ireland information controversy followed information controversy.

In many ways the debate which I hope we will have here is at a higher level than that in Britain. The issues that we will speak about – freedom of information, official secrecy, accountability, corruption in business and in government – are nevertheless similar issues often based on the same laws as those across the water.

But there it is difficult to focus on those issues because of the concerns with the activities of the tabloid press. In Britain the particular focus on scandal, on the Royals and on politician's private lives is a function of intense competition between media magnates who have more or less monopolised the markets, feeding off a scabrous tradition in British culture which is based on the class structure in that society.

At this conference, however, we will not focus directly on journalistic standards, which are in fact high in Ireland. Yet the paradox is that, despite those high standards, the same restrictions, and indeed in some ways more restrictions, apply here than apply in Britain.

There have been meetings before in Ireland, on aspects of the subject of censorship, but as far as I am aware this is the first occasion on which there is an effort to treat comprehensively all aspects of this subject.

The underlying theme of our deliberations will be very straightforward: the subject of information and its role in a democratic society. The international standard which is binding on this country, and which, therefore, is the benchmark by which we should want to judge ourselves, speaks of everyone's right "to seek, to receive, to impart information and ideas of all kinds through any media, regardless of frontiers, either orally, in writing, or in print, in the form of art, or through any media of choice". And our focus, I would suggest, in the presentations and in the workshops should be to ask whether we measure up to that international standard. And if, indeed, everything was rosy we would in fact be meeting in a pub. The presence of the enormous numbers at this meeting makes clear that in many areas we do not measure up very well to this particular standard which is binding on our government.

The purpose of our conference is to ask what can be done about the failures, the weaknesses of our system, and more particularly, what are *we* going to do about it, because this conference is concerned not only to debate but to plan for action to ensure that we achieve this international standard.

This conference is being held at the end, or perhaps not at the end, of an extraordinary period of Irish public life where the country seems to be preoccupied with little else than the rights and wrongs of concealing information, of attempting to give information and attempting to seek information.

Over this last year we have seen apparently endless conflicts between citizens and the state over governmental interference with information – conflicts which involved local and international courts and which made world news in the case of the X case. Let me just briefly review the issues. The first one's rather a sad one. The European Commission on Human Rights dismissed a challenge to Section 31 of the Broadcasting Act in April 1991, a sore point since I was involved as a lawyer in that case. The legal battle over the broadcasting ban has returned to Ireland on an issue not relating to the legality of the ban, but as to whom it applies to.

The European Court of Justice, the EC Court in Luxembourg, upheld an injunction on the provision of abortion information by students, within Ireland, an injunction which another European Court, the European Court of Human Rights, held to be in conflict with the Convention on Human Rights. That saga on abortion information continues following the referendum in which the people voted to ensure information, a decision which is awaiting implementation through legislation from the new government – promised, though no detail has been given, in the programme for government.

We have had a series of business scandals – Telecom, Greencore and Goodman, which of course has led to the Beef Tribunal. Behind this bewildering array of scandals has been a confusing mixture of unaccountable private and public power – business people, state servants, politicians – operating with all the advantages of secrecy that the law of libel and other laws and the government culture in this society present and offer.

The Beef Tribunal itself, established to get at the truth, has left us with more challenges to freedom of information. The Supreme Court has ruled, apparently, that all documents emanating from the cabinet are confidential and no one seems to understand how far this doctrine goes, though in my opinion *The Irish Times,* among other Irish newspapers, has gone over the top in their own interpretation of the case. I don't think it is as serious as it looks.

The issue of journalistic privacy has come up in the Beef Tribunal in classic style. The journalist who discovered the alleged corruption and whose work led to the establishment of the tribunal now could be punished because she refuses to give her sources. Susan O'Keefe is the journalist, the messenger being the focus of attention and punishment rather than the message that is emerging from that tribunal. Meanwhile, to complete this list of incidents, the long established paternalism of this state over what we can read continues with the banning of Madonna's book *Sex.* It may not be great literature, but it is absurd that the law should be used to ban books in this state in the 1990s.

All of these different aspects of governmental interference with freedom of information will then be the subject of our conference. And I would like to say that this is not a conference for the press or, as such, about the press. Information belongs to the public and to the whole population and is a vital resource for that citizenry. The theme of our conference is censorship and secrecy in a democratic society, not the occupational hazards of journalism.

It is of course a well-timed conference, coming as it does when a new government is about to take power, a government which has declared itself to be committed to openness, integrity, accountability at the highest level of democratic participation. Wonderful and important commitments which we will look forward to seeing delivered. Objectives which can be applauded. But we can also be critical as well as encouraging of the new administration.

The slogan adopted for this conference is one that we should remember, "Let in the Light". Because it was the present Taoiseach, Albert Reynolds, who less than a year ago, when he was about to enter another coalition as leader, proclaimed that "we will let in the light".

Well, we didn't see much evidence of it in the intervening months and he knows now that he has another chance with his Labour partners to do precisely that. Before this conference was convened a public statement was published in *The Irish Times* and signed by 200-odd people and it called for a public debate on a number of issues. Firstly, on the reform of the Official Secrets Act and the enactment of a freedom of information act containing a positive assertion of the right to information. What does the joint Programme for Government of Labour and Fianna Fáil say on that matter? Well, it says as follows: "We will consider the introduction of freedom of information legislation." A commitment which is not particularly strong and is indeed extremely disappointing.

No mention is made of the Official Secrets Act. It is a measure of the task of this conference that, whatever action follows it, we must encourage the government to make this consideration of the introduction of a freedom of information act one which will translate into an actual freedom of information act.

The basic point about the freedom of information act is this: it shifts the balance of power between the government and the governed; between the state and the citizen. It means that government begins on the assumption that all information generated by government belongs to the people, not to public representatives, nor to the permanent government, the civil servants. There should be no concept in a democracy of secrecy.

There should, of course, be a concept of protected information. All freedom of information acts across the world protect, alongside access to information, privacy and categories of information of importance in the general interest which should not be available. The assumption should be that all information should be available.

On the censorship of publications, of films and the arts – another concern in the public statement – there is nothing to report in the document of government. It seems that we are likely to continue with the panoply of publications, film and video censorship.

Political censorship through the Offences Against the State Act and in Section 31 of the Broadcasting Act was obviously an expression of concern in the public statement. The programme for government is silent on the subject, but I understand we should know soon the government position.

The Section 31 order has been renewed annually every January for the past sixteen years with no debate, and against the protest of civil liberty bodies and journalists. The question is, will it be renewed next week?

It could at the least be asked that the new minister, Michael D. Higgins – if he considers that he needs to confirm this order because he has not had opportunity to consider the implications of its removal – should renew it for a shorter period, not twelve months. Perhaps three months, for example – a period which would allow him to undertake what has never been done, a thorough review of the ban and to take into account the opinions of those who have to work the censorship in RTE.

The need for accountability in the business and commercial world is another concern of the statement. It is something which is in part dealt with in the promises of the new government, in the Ethics in Government Bill, the register of members' interests and the extension of that to senior civil servants. It does not, however, deal with the question of secrecy, corruption and lack of integrity in private business, and the need to ensure openness in corporate practices in this country.

The need for full access to medical and reproductive information was another concern mentioned in the public statement. It finds some response in the programme for government where regulation is promised to implement this right to information flowing from the recent abortion referendum. Again we must wait to see what is actually produced by way of regulation, and we must salute the women who have led this campaign against the most ugly face of censorship of all of the recent episodes in this country. It was the clinics, the women's clinics, and the students who were hauled through the courts and who ensured that the absurd situation of injuncting the imparting of information to other women was ended. The law that is passed must be one that restores completely the fundamental right of women to seek information on abortion through any media, regardless of frontiers.

Carl Bernstein

LET ME BEGIN by saying something about who I am and who I'm not. I'm a reporter, a journalist, a writer, not a historian or a philosopher; so, as informally as possible, I'd like to talk about reporting in the press and share some impressions with you about what is happening in the media today, particularly in the English-speaking world.

The theme of this conference is "Censorship, Secrecy and Democracy". You are going to have the opportunity to hear presentations that I hope will leave no doubt that none of us is truly free until each of us is free to speak and write and read what we choose, without intimidation, without fear of arrest, without fear of censorship. Without fear of terrorism, I should also add, the absence of which is also an essential element of human freedom and the democratic condition.

The idea that, at the close of the 20th century, we find it necessary to convene in the land of Swift, Burke, Joyce and Beckett to address such fundamental matters of human rights and intellectual freedom as we're discussing here is itself a terrible indictment. And just as damning is the fact that across the Irish Sea the British government, at a moment when the economy and society of Britain face the gravest questions, is utterly preoccupied with the debate over further censorship of the press and finding ways to put more teeth into its already draconian information policies.

In the former capitals of the Soviet empire, this appalling state of affairs might be conceivable, perhaps. Yet in most of those capitals today, the right of the people to read and write and publish and broadcast as they choose is greater than that in Dublin and London.

One of the things that's always bothered me the most about the press is our pretention of omniscience – the attitude that somehow, because we're journalists or reporters, we're all-knowing, that we have all the answers. So I begin by sharing with you my view that's it's time for the press to begin finding some humility, to recognise not only our immense power but the responsibilities that go with it, and remember the simple fact that we're human, we're fallible, we make mistakes frequently. We need to acknowledge them when we make them, and this might be an hour in which it is particularly appropriate to acknowledge that our profession is in unusual trouble and in danger of losing its way.

Arriving in Britain in the week of the publication of the Camillagate tapes, one would have no apprehensions of anything approaching even humility or commitment to what good reporting, good journalism, really is – "the best obtainable version of the truth". And I'm going to return again to that most basic definition of what reporting really is because in Britain, as in America, and here too I sense, we're losing sight of that ideal.

In its place we're seeing the dominance of a journalistic culture that has little to do with the truth or reality or context. Increasingly the picture of our societies, as rendered in our media today, is illusionary and delusionary. It is disfigured, unreal, out of touch with the truth, disconnected from the truth, disconnected from the true context of our lives, disfigured by celebrity, by celebrity worship, by gossip, by sensationalism, by denial of our society's real condition and by a political and social discourse that we, the press, the media, politicians and the people, are turning into a sewer.

The sponsors of this conference have asked me to talk about the relationship between freedom of information and how it empowers people. I can't think of a more appropriate topic. Today in Britain the government stands ready yet again to move against the press and further restrict its ability to report the truth. Again, as in Watergate in America, the authorities are making the conduct of the press the issue, rather than the conduct of those who govern. And I can think, of course, of innumerable instances where the people in America particularly have been empowered by the absence of an official secrets act such as the British and Irish press suffer under. Indeed I would argue that the most fundamental basis of American freedom and liberty is the First Amendment to our Constitution, which gives us the right to absolute free speech and a free press.

From the beginning, the First Amendment has given voice to the empowerment of our people, even those in society with the least power, and through our history the courts have upheld and even broadened the meaning of the First Amendment. It's doubtful that the great reporting from Vietnam would have survived your

Official Secrets Act, or Britain's. Certainly the Pentagon Papers could never have been published without prior judicial restraint and official review in Ireland or Britain, yet there was nothing in the publication of those terribly important documents that endangered national security. Certainly with an official secrets act our reporting in Watergate would have been met with government attempts to shut us down, although the secrets of Watergate had nothing to do with genuine national concerns either, only with a criminal presidency.

In fact, I have yet to see a single instance of a true violation of real strategic secrets in America, in Britain, or in Europe, despite all the talk of it. I can think of innumerable instances in which we in the press have been entrusted with military and secret information which we handled responsibly and did not disclose.

We're not a danger to national security but, rather, a danger sometimes to the interests of those in power. And I'm sure that, quite correctly, much of this conference will dwell on the culture of secrecy that Ireland has inherited from the British civil service, from the Church, from a tradition of literary and press censorship.

But I'd like to suggest that the real way to break through a culture of secrecy is to challenge it with the power of our work – as Joyce did, as Beckett did, as Swift did. Go out and do the reporting, write the books, write the stories, make the films, write the plays, publish the broadsheets and then, after the reporting, after the hard work of looking at the human condition and examining it has been done, after the writing has been done, if it runs up then against an official secrets act or some other form of censorship, then let's cross that bridge strongly and forcibly when the time comes, armed with the power of our work – as Joyce did, as Beckett did, as Swift did. Because, most of the time these days, we journalists, in particular, are not even on the road towards the bridge, much less ready to cross it. Because we're not doing the basic work of our profession, the hard business of reporting and searching for the truth, for relevance, for context, for accuracy: "the best obtainable version of the truth".

So, I would also like to speak about how the misuse of the freedom of information disempowers people. Because I believe that the appalling condition of much of our journalism today on both sides of the Atlantic has more to do with our own abdication of responsibility than it does with government secrecy or the attempt, which we must continually fight, to limit our access to information and our ability to publish it. We need to be looking first at our performance.

The truth is, we limit ourselves more often than government limits us, because we're not willing to do the hard work in searching out the truth. It's difficult, very difficult. It takes a lot of effort, a lot of time, but it's not our priority any more in journalism. Increasingly we journalists don't have enough courage to give our readers and viewers what we know is real news. Instead, we pander to them, even occasionally in the best of our newspapers, in the best of our broadcasts. And keep in mind that the standards of the best – the *New York Times* or the *Washington Post*, or the *Financial Times*, the *Sunday Times,* the *Wall Street Journal* – these are hardly the standards of most of our journalism in the English-speaking world.

Over the last 20 years we've been abdicating our primary function – "the best obtainable version of the truth" – and allowing our agenda and priorities to become bastardised and dominated by what I called last year, in an article in the *New Republic* published in the *Guardian* on this side of the Atlantic, "the triumph of idiot culture".

Make no mistake about who the most influential figure in journalism in the past quarter century is: not Catherine Graham of the *Washington Post*, or Ben Bradlee, or Abe Rosenthal of the *New York Times*, or the director general of the BBC or the team from CBS News' *Sixty Minutes*. The most influential figure in journalism in the last quarter century is Rupert Murdoch. I think it's time for those of us who work in the news media to recognise that Rupert Murdoch and the gutter standards of the low end of his empire, which increasingly are affecting the standards even of the high end of our business, is an even greater threat to the truth than an official secrets act.

His influence – and I'm using Mr Murdoch here as something of a metaphor, for today we have dozens of Murdochs in our journalistic culture – and the standards he adheres to are much more to do with what people read and see than any restrictive legislation in any of our countries. The gravest threat, I believe, may well be from within our own profession. Because the consequences to a society, misinformed and disinformed by the grotesque values of a Murdoch culture, are truly perilous. Today in journalism we are perhaps in danger of really, irrevocably disgracing ourselves, or, at least passively, allowing the huge media companies to disgrace us by erasing the distinctions between real journalism – "the best obtainable version of the truth" – and this ravenous celebrity-sensation-and scandal-machine that's consuming decent journalism and relegating truth and real reporting to an anachronistic adjunct of a kind of new pornography journalism.

It is an adjunct used by many of our giant media corporations, and this includes corporations that own some of our greatest newspapers and broadcasting outlets, allowing them to clothe themselves in respectability as increasingly they make their real money off trash – trash TV, trash book publishing, trash magazines, trash news.

Let me read you something from an American newspaper:

"Hotel records show that Maples paid no bills".

That's from the front page of *Newsday*, one of our better newspapers. That day the whole front page of *Newsday* was devoted to the story of the break-up of the marriage of Donald Trump, an American financier and builder, his wife Ivana, and the role of Mr Trump's girlfriend, Marla Maples. It was also the same day that story occupied the front page of *Newsday* that Nelson Mandela returned to Soweto after his years in the South African gulag, and the day on which the allies of World War II agreed to the unification of Germany. Those stories were inside the paper. That's the triumph of idiot culture.

Perhaps the gravest triumph of idiot culture is to be found on television, on American talk-shows, and now their British and European counterparts.

Again, the same cast: "Tell me, Marla, was it really the best sex you ever had?" The words are of Diane Sawyer, one of our top journalists, on the first edition of the much heralded ABC TV news show, *Prime Time Live*.

The hypocrisy of the British press this week is a thing to behold. You'd have thought that the English-speaking world had been saved by the British press. And that there would be no further erosion of press freedom because truth, and justice, and honesty, and the people's right to know has not only been served but prevailed as a result of the publication of the Royals' bugged telephone conversation... The greatest triumph of democracy, we would be led to believe by the self-satisfied editorials in almost every British newspaper this week.

Truth, I think we know here, is often complex. The best obtainable version of the truth is about context. And this is perhaps the greatest single failing of our journalism today. Far too much of it, maybe even most of it, is utterly without context.

Facts by themselves are not truth. Thus the gossip press, the Murdoch press, even when they occasionally have a fact or two right, often are a form of misinformation because their aim is to shock, to titillate, to distort, to give grotesque emphasis. Standards of the gossip columns are soaring careers one day, crash and burn the next. They're not the standards of real life, which is really about grey, about complexity, about texture.

That's what our journalism should be about, just as our literature aims towards that. Yes, we need protection against being forced in court to name our sources. Yes, we need disclosure laws that will shine a light on political financing in Ireland, Britain and America. But I come back to my central point. The darkness and the secrecy is largely of our creation, because we have chosen not to shine the light of reporting and honest, difficult enquiry on the institutions and conditions of our societies.

If one hundredth of the reportorial effort expended on the private lives of the Prince and Princess of Wales were assigned to real news, important news, relevant news, Britain would be a different kind of country. With a much better informed public, with debates in the pub about its economic future, the question of Ireland, the future of its school system, the relevance of the class system, instead of a public discourse that, as in America, has been poisoned by the lurid and loopy standards that we see with the Murdochs and the Oprah Winfreys and Donohues in America. We have a talk-show nation, a talk-show culture.

Should there be any form of non-military censorship except for genuine secrets of national security which are already adequately protected by the laws of espionage and treason? Of course not. Not for the press. Not for doctors, and health workers who want to counsel abortion. Not for anyone... Madonna's book was recently banned here by the Censorship of Publications Board. But there's hardly a major media company today, in Britain or in America, or in Western Europe, that hasn't dipped its toe in the journalistic equivalent of porn, either through books or television shows. And, meanwhile, they try to occupy in the culture a sacrosanct position by publishing up-market, stately, responsible newspapers while making more money off the bottom, pornographic end of journalism.

But the real shame is that those of us that are "responsible" journalists and writers have not resisted, have not said to our editors and publishers: "Enough! You are endangering the credibility of all our work." Instead of trying to isolate the Murdochs of journalism we join them and welcome their standards to our own pages and broadcasts, pretending that we "respectable" journalists are somehow in a different corner. There's nothing respectable about our position unless we draw a line that says we're different, reject the Murdoch agenda, and, by publicly rejecting his gutter approach, perhaps our viewers and readers may feel a bit ashamed in continuing to wallow in this effluent.

For more than 15 years we've been moving away from real journalism and towards the creation of a sleazoid, gossip culture in which the lines between the decent and indecent are often indistinguishable. We teach our readers and viewers the trivial and insignificant. The lurid and the loopy are more important than real news. We don't serve our readers and viewers, but pander to them, and we condescend to them, giving them what we think they want, what we calculate will sell and boost our ratings and readership. Many of them, sadly, seem to justify our condescension and seem to revel in the trash.

Nevertheless, it's the role of journalists, writers, intellectuals, to challenge people, not to merely amuse them. We're in the process of creating the idiot culture – not an idiot subculture, which every society has bubbling beneath the surface, which can be harmless, but the culture itself. For the first time in our history the weird, the stupid, and the coarse are becoming our cultural norm, even our cultural ideal. In America, radio and television shows which thrive on race-baiting and intolerance, manufactured controversy, are the most popular broadcasts on the air.

Even the *New York Times* is being influenced. It has been reduced to naming the rape victim in the William Kennedy Smith case; to putting trash biographer Kitty Kelley on page one as a news story; to purveying, as the *Washington Post* and other publications do, political polls as if they were really about substantive policy.

Until our recent election the agenda of the talk-show nation had become the agenda of American discourse, an idiot agenda that bears little relevance to the real problems of our country. And, of course, an idiot culture is an escapist culture. It's designed to take us away from what we need to be examining. But there was something about this election in America in November: I believe it was a combination of the economy and George Bush's obsessive and continuous lying, not just about the economic conditions of the country but about himself, his own record, even simple things that could have easily elicited a truthful response. His excess finally put much of the American press back on the track of real news. At least for a while.

So I think George Bush is right when he blamed the press largely for his defeat, or at least partially right, because we did get back towards the ideal of the best obtainable version of the truth. We forced ourselves finally to go back and look at the reality of our condition and measure it against the words of our President, and measure it against the record of our President.

Today, the most compelling news story in the world, I believe, is the condition of the post-communist West. Our political system is in deep crisis, we are witnessing in each of our societies a breakdown of the community that, in the past, allowed post-war democracy to build and progress. Surely the advent of idiot culture journalism is part of the breakdown. Some good journalism is still being done today, to be sure, but increasingly, I think, it's the exception not the rule in the English-speaking world and on the continent as well.

Good journalism today requires a kind of courage that it never did before, to go against the tide, a quality now in scarce supply in our mass media. Much of our social welfare system, our educational system, needs to be challenged, and, more than anything, I think some of our assumptions about the media itself, about the culture of information itself, have to be challenged.

For the story of the contemporary Western media is the great uncovered story today. We need to start asking ourselves the same fundamental questions about the press, about information, about publishing, about broadcasting, that we do of other powerful institutions in our society. About who is served, about standards, about self-interests. For the reality is the media are probably the most powerful and most influential of all our institutions today – more powerful and influential, really, than our political institutions.

They are squandering their immense power, and ignoring their obligations, or more precisely we are, who abdicated our responsibilities. And the consequence of our abdication is the spectacle of the triumph and tragedy of idiot culture in a time when we need truth and reality. So I think now this conference is a good place to talk about the process of reform, but not just reform in government, which we also need, but beginning in our own house.

Salman Rushdie

THE LAST TIME I came to Dublin was a few years ago when I'd written a novel called *The Satanic Verses*. I came and talked to literary journalists and did readings in bookshops and signed copies of the book, and nobody seemed to think it was anything other than a novel. Including me.

I hope the moment might arise shortly when it goes back to being a novel instead of whatever the hell else it has become.

I guess what I wanted to start off by saying is that one way or another I seem to have been bumping into censors and censorship most of my life as a writer, and not just as a writer, because there was a point in my life when I thought I might be an actor.

Mercifully the world was spared, but not the whole world, because when I left university I went back to Pakistan where my parents were by this time living, a bad mistake of theirs. I found myself there at a loose end after having graduated from Cambridge and they had just opened a television station in Karachi for the first time. I was looking around for some work and I managed to persuade the head of the Karachi television station to let me coproduce and act in a production of Edward Albee's play *The Zoo Story*.

They did one English-language programme a night, usually *Dallas*, and so I suggested that instead of buying a programme, why didn't they make one. They liked *The Zoo Story* because it had a cast of two. The set was a park bench and it was 45 minutes long. On this basis they agreed to do it, but I then had to submit the text to the controllers of Pakistan television and there followed a really deeply surrealist series of conversations.

There's a scene, a very long monologue, in *The Zoo Story* played by a character called Gerry who has most of the lines, and so I decided to play Gerry. In the monologue he talks about living in a house with his horrible landlady who has a very savage dog, and he tries to make friends with the dog. The dog attacks him every time he comes home, so before he passes by the dog he goes to the corner shop and buys the dog six hamburgers. He comes home, throws down the six hamburgers and the dog rejects the hamburgers and attacks him.

And he says – the line in the play is Albee's, not mine – "I don't know why he didn't eat the hamburgers, they were six perfectly good hamburgers with not enough pork in them to make them disgusting."

At this point the head of Pakistan television leaned across his desk and said to me, "The word 'pork' cannot be spoken on Pakistan television."

So I said: "Look, why not? This speech is excellent anti-pork propaganda. This speech says pork makes hamburgers so disgusting that dogs won't eat them."

At which point he then put to me, "You see, pork is a four-letter word." Which was true, but so was ham and so was bacon. So we had to cut the reference to the pork.

Later on, when Gerry gets past the dog, the landlady assaults him. She doesn't bite him, she tries to do other things – well, biting might have been involved – but she attempts to assault him on the landing and she rubs her body against him.

There's a section of the monologue in which a sexual assault by the landlady is described in great detail. During the course of this description the word sex is mentioned three times. The head of Pakistan television said to me, "This sex is a four-letter word."

So I said: "Well, it's not possible to delete this speech because it's crucial. You don't know what happens in the play if you don't understand the landlady is trying to attack him sexually."

"The scene is fine," he said, "but the word sex is not fine."

We replace the word sex on one occasion with "lust", on another with "desire", and on a third occasion with "love". Then the scene was fine.

This was an early experience of censorship, but, at about the same time, a cinema in Karachi called the Bambino had recently opened which was famous for its gigantic screen. As their opening movie, they had hired the Charlton Heston film, *El Cid*, but there was a scandal when Pakistani censors watched the film. They saw it all the way to the end when they saw this terrifying thing happened. In the penultimate scene El Cid rides out to battle against the Arabs and is mortally wounded. He comes back home dying. He lies in his castle and when he dies his dead body is strapped to a horse and goes out and defeats the Muslims.

The idea that the dead body of a Christian soldier could defeat a Muslim army was not acceptable, and, as a result, the censors banned the film. Consternation. Who was going to come and watch all this stereo equipment if there was no film to show?

Eventually a compromise was found. The last scene was cut from the film so that the film now ended with the scene in which El Cid went out to battle, was mortally wounded, came back, and died in the arms of Sophia Loren. End of movie with the right result.

This is what happens in the world of censorship. I remember another movie, Richard Attenborough's extremely bad film *Ghandi*, which contains, amongst other things, a version of the founder of Pakistan, Muhammad Ali Jinnah, who is portrayed more or less as Count Dracula. It is not a flattering portrait, and, as a result, the film was banned in Pakistan amidst a certain amount of fuss.

Various people said that maybe it should be allowed in, and, eventually, the major newspaper in Pakistan ran a lead editorial in which they said "certain liberal elements in our society had been suggesting that this film *Ghandi* should be shown so that people can make up their own minds. If these people were not so liberal," it said, "they might be better citizens of Pakistan."

One of the corruptions of life in a dictatorship, of life in total censorship, is that people lose the ability to understand the meaning of their own sentences. Whoever wrote that editorial thought he was making a serious point – which he was – but it was not the point he thought he was making.

Pakistani television is of course these days dominated by priests. One of the most popular jokes about this in Pakistan is the story of a man who buys himself a new television set, switches it on, and a few hours later sends for the repair man. The repair man comes round and asks what the problem is. The owner says, "Well, the television isn't working properly. Can you fix it please?"

So he switches on the television and the repair man says: "There's the picture, it's fine, what's your problem?"

And the owner of the TV set says, "Look there's this picture of this mullah that has got stuck in the television. Can you get it off please? Can we not see some other picture?"

When one has a background where censorship is normal, it becomes very depressing when one comes to a part of the world where it is not normal, and yet where you hear people providing all kinds of fantastically plausible and good reasons for it. You know... censorship to protect this or that interest group, to defend people against sensibilities, and one or two journalists have actually said things like this to me today.

It's very hard to say to them, "Look, you guys never lived in the end product of the argument that you're talking about. It's all right for you. You think you can give away one per cent of your freedom and you've still got 99 per cent, but actually, once you give away the first one per cent it's very remarkable how fast the other 99 per cent goes."

I've been talking about Pakistan, but I wouldn't like to let India off the hook. India allows the press to be free because nobody can read. The broadcast media, television and radio, are very heavily censored, and it is absolutely commonplace for the main television news to have to yank off the lead item because some minister has rung up and said "you can't run that", and to have to insert instead a word-for-word recitation of the minister's request for what they should say.

I became friendly at one time with the managing director of programmes of India Television whose main claim to fame was that he had introduced a serious innovation into Indian news broadcasting – when a major news event was happening to which television cameras were sent, he had the idea that he might also send a reporter along. That was his innovation, and as a result, six months after he decided that maybe journalists could go to news events, he was fired.

India believes that you must control the airwaves – in a country of 15 per cent literacy you can allow the press to be free. It doesn't matter.

I had a strange experience of this sort in 1987 when I went to India for its 40th anniversary celebrations and at that time made a documentary about the state of the nation. We went to Kashmir where it became quite clear that every single person that we talked to, without exception – that is 100 per cent of those we talked to – wished to secede from India. And yet there was not a single political party in India or in Kashmir which was willing to say that was the case.

I remember talking to people about this who said so, with absolute unanimity, and then the television camera would start running and they would say no, we all absolutely love the democratic system of India. When the camera stopped running, I would say, "Why do you say that? You've just been telling me something else for two hours." And they pointed out to me that there was an eleven-year jail sentence for anyone who dared to criticize the union with India.

This creates a problem. After making this sequence of film I went back to Delhi and I was talking to my left-wing, progressive, libertarian friends. I would say, "Do you realise that 100 per cent of the people of Kashmir want to secede from India?"

And they said, "You mustn't talk like that. That's sectarian communalist pro-Muslim language."

"Actually, it's not," I said, "it's what we call the truth."

And they said, "You know, you've been away too long. You don't understand the situation."

Five years later Kashmir explodes and the left-wing, progressive, libertarian voices of India want to know what the hell happened.

This is another effect of censorship. People begin to believe the censored version. They internalise it. And then they criticise you for saying that something else is the case. In the same film I met and filmed a woman, a Sikh woman, who had been the victim of religious violence – after the murder of Indira Ghandi an enormous holocaust had been unleashed against Indian Sikhs because they were supposed to be involved in the murder. There's lots of evidence to show that the Indian Congress Party was involved in those murders.

The woman we talked to was a woman whose husband and children had been burnt to death in front of her. She was a very strong woman but seriously, as you would imagine, damaged. She was strong enough, however, that she wished to talk to us, knowing the risk she was incurring in going up against the government of India, for the very simple reason that she just wanted the story to be told. That's all. "I want people to be told what happened when they killed my family," she said. So we recorded her, and there then developed the most enormous, god-almighty row with the Indian embassy in London whom we had undertaken to show the film to.

They accused us of all kinds of things, threatened many things, and rang the television station to demand that the film should be pulled. And I said to them, "Look, what we're talking about here is a victim of terrorism. We're not talking about a terrorist. We are talking about a woman who has seen her whole life destroyed by a violent mob in front of her house, and you're telling me that you, as a democratic country, refuse her the right to speak. This is a woman who, during her testimony, expressly distances herself from all forms of Sikh violence.

"She says she is not interested in the Sikh movement for a separatist state, she just wants people to know that mobs killed her family."

The Indian government attempted to prevent this from happening. We showed the film anyway, but it became very difficult for that film company to make subsequent films in India.

I guess I'm coming round to saying what I suppose I have come here to say because, in various ways, all these are incidents of the arrival of religion in the arena of what can be said and what can be thought, or the cloak of religion used to disguise what are in fact political events.

So I thought I should talk a little bit about how things stand between God and me. Not very well. Shortly after the Khomeni *fatwa* I was sent a tee-shirt by an American reader of the book which had on the front of it the legend "Blasphemy is a victimless crime," and I thought that was a text worth considering.

(I also wanted just to mention that – certainly in the British political system – blasphemy is not a crime against the church, it is a crime against the state. That's to say the law of blasphemy is part of the law of seditious libel and what you are doing when you blaspheme is to attack the state. This is because, of course, England has an established church, and to attack the established church is to attack the church of the Queen and no doubt the Prince of Wales and his friends.)

I'm in favour of blasphemy. I'd just like to say a little bit about why that should be so. I'm going to say something that got me into a lot of trouble in Washington. I was in Washington last year at the time when we finally managed to publish the paperback of *The Satanic Verses* and I was at a conference, not unlike this, convened for reasons not unlike these, to talk about these subjects. I said at that conference that the problem with believing that blasphemy is something that should be prevented is that the three most important trials in the history of western culture were all blasphemy trials – the trial of Jesus Christ, the trial of Socrates and the trial of Galileo.

All these three men were tried for blasphemy and found guilty. So that if one accepts that blasphemy is a limiting point on thought, you would at that point unmake western morality and philosophy and western science. This is amongst the reasons I am in favour of blasphemy. At the point at which I said this, or shortly afterwards, a Russian gentleman in the audience – his first name was Melor and the reason he's called Melor is that it stands for Marx, Engels, Lenin, October Revolution – Mr Marx Engels Lenin October Revolution stood up and said, "How dare you compare yourself to Jesus Christ?"

I said, "What?"

And he replied, "You think you're as good as Socrates or Galileo. What an arrogant man!"

I said, "Excuse me, I was making a different point." And, anyway, this gentleman worked for *Izvestia*, an organisation which on the subject of free speech ought to be reasonably modest.

So at the risk of being accused of comparing myself to Jesus Christ, I would like to mention that blasphemy was what He did, and also what Socrates did, and what Galileo did. And I must say I have often thought in these mad years of Galileo's reputedly muttered words at the point at which he recanted his idea that the earth went round the sun, the point at which he had to stand before the servants of God and recant, this famous phrase that he used under his breath: "*Eppur si muove*" – "Actually, it does move".

Moving on from Jesus, Socrates and Galileo, I think it's important also to remember that the group of writers that we now call the European Enlightenment were writers who were in revolt, not against the state, but against the Church, and that the boundaries they sought to widen were widened by a deliberate use of blasphemy. And lest we feel too smug about what they did, it's worth remembering that almost none of their books could be published during their lifetime. The *Confessions* of Rousseau was not published in his lifetime. The same is true of Diderot's *Jacques de Fataliste*.

When Voltaire said that it was preferable for writers to live near frontiers so that if they got into trouble they could skip across, he wasn't talking about trouble with the state, he was talking about trouble with the Church. That remark of Voltaire's actually calls to mind Joyce's famous remark about what writers require: "Silence, exile and cunning." Well, silence doesn't seem to be very effective these days. Exile doesn't work because they come after you. This leaves cunning. So I think what we need now is cunning and cunning.

To come to the present and *The Satanic Verses*: one of the things that people have attempted to say about this case is that it is in some way a conflict between western and eastern values; that, somehow, the west stands for freedom and the east stands for un-freedom. I think that this is a kind of caricature of what's hap-pening because there exists inside all third world countries, inside all Muslim countries, exactly the same battles between freedom and unfreedom as those that exist between the west and the east, or indeed within the west, except that in the east the power is all in the hands of the forces of unfreedom.

It's worth mentioning that Islam has not managed to create a free society anywhere in the world, ever in human history. Iranian writers, Iranian intellectuals, writers, philosophers, scientists in exile, who now comprise all the most distinguished Iranian intel-lectuals that exist, well understand what has been done in the case of *The Satanic Verses*. They well understand that my fight is also their fight, and that's why they have been among the most coura-geous and vociferous groups in defending me.

Earlier last year there was a statement from 60 or 70 of the most prominent of them in which they made the very important point that blasphemy cannot anymore be considered to be a limiting point on thought. Because if it is, then you reinvent the Inquisition. You unmake the Enlightenment and you put power back into the hands of Savonarola and Torquemada. You put power back into the hands of the witch-finder general.

And I'm sure many of you remember the story of the witch-finder general, Matthew Hopkins, in the time of Cromwell. He seemed to work mostly in East Anglia and his main technique for finding a witch was to load her down with stones and throw her into the river. If she sank she was not a witch, but if she floated she was a witch, in which case, of course, she would burn. Various writers – Norman Cohen, Marina Warner, and others – have analysed the phenomenon of witchcraft and they point out what are the identifying signs of a witch: she has a pointed hat – very common in England in the 17th century! She has a cat, the most common domestic animal. She has a magic broom such as would be found in any woman's kitchen, and she has the witch's nipple. That's to say she has a mole on her chest. These are all entirely commonplace domestic objects such as any woman in the 17th century would have possessed. That's to say, anybody is a witch if somebody points at them and says "witch".

And that's what happened in the great witch-hunt of the 17th century in which it now seems clear there were almost no witches. East Anglia was not a great centre for witchcraft. There were no covens. What there were were difficult women, unpopular in villages, and a witch-finder to come and find them. And their neighbours, and the people who didn't like them, those who thought they didn't fit in the neighbourhood, pointed at these women and said "witch".

The next thing they knew they were being weighed down with stones and thrown into the river to see if they floated. Well, that's what's happening again, that's what's happened to me.

Somebody pointed across the world and said "witch". And you know, I may not have a pointed hat but I have a hat, and I don't have a cat but I might. I probably have a mole. I certainly have a broomstick, so that's me done for. And that's how it goes.

That's what happens when laws like blasphemy and heresy are unleashed into the world. These are the most evil laws in the human race because they are the laws which put shackles on our thoughts. And they need fighting as hard as possible and in every form that they crop up. So instead of saying, "I'm sorry, I didn't mean to be blasphemous," if you think it's blasphemous, so what? Who gives you the right to say that because something is blasphemous it should not be said?

I felt very early on that the problem didn't lie between me and God. Put very simply, if there is a God I doubt very much if he is particularly bothered about *The Satanic Verses*, because what sort of a God would be bothered about a novel? On the other hand, if there is no God, he clearly is not worried about *The Satanic Verses*. In either case it seems to me that the dispute is not between me and God, but between me and people who, as Bob Dylan used to say, kill people because they have God on their side.

I just want to go on and talk a little bit about the question of whether there are limits to free speech, whether free speech is an absolute or not. And I have to say that in this regard my mind has changed somewhat. I used to spend a lot of the '70s working in race relations in England, and, certainly at that time, I would have been a defender of the British Race Relations Act and believed in legislation making racist speech illegal.

Since then I've thought a great deal about this. I've listened to the arguments of American thinkers such as Ronald Dworkin and Noam Chomsky, who would argue that it is incorrect to limit speech at the point at which it becomes revoltingly unpleasant. One has to say it's no trick to agree with people's right to say things that you broadly speaking think are decent and civilised. The point about the freedom of speech is to allow uncivilised discourse. And to understand that it is a necessary evil if you are going to have any of the freedom that you actually want.

It's easy to argue that I would say this, wouldn't I. But, oddly, the reason I've come to this conclusion does not have to do with my desire to go around insulting people, it has actually rather more to do with what I have learnt about the phenomenon of people insulting me.

A few years ago there was a television film made, a Pakistani television film called *International Guerrillas*. The subject of *International Guerrillas* was the heroic attempt by Islamic terrorists to murder me. In this film there was a character called Salman Rushdie, who was presented as being a drunkard, a sadist, a torturer and a murderer, and at the end of the film this character was murdered by no less a person than God. The international guerrillas having failed to reach their target, it was time for direct action.

I watched this film. It was appalling and one of the things I most objected to was the fact that the character playing me appeared in a very large assortment of incredibly ugly safari suits, cerise safari suits, and other equally unpleasant colours. But there is something undeniably revolting about watching yourself being murdered by God in the movies.

This film was offered for release in England and the British Board of Film Classifications refused it a certificate, so it was banned. This then resulted in the most extraordinary kind of looking glass event in which I was obliged to write to the British Board of Film Classifications telling them that I would not proceed in any way legally against this film, telling them that I did not wish the protection of censorship and would they please give this film a licence.

As a direct result of this request the film was given a licence and was released, and what then happened was an extraordinary and rather impressive demonstration of the value of free speech. Had this film been banned it would have become a *cause célebre*, it would have become the video hot ticket. The film was released. The distributors, with great pride, booked the biggest cinema in Bradford, the heart of the British Muslim community, and opened the movie and were greeted by row after row of empty seats. Nobody went. Within two days the film was taken off and the distributors had made a colossal loss. Even people who didn't like *The Satanic Verses*, or what they'd been told about it, didn't want to go and watch a rotten movie.

It's a very difficult thing to come to the conclusion that what you believe is that people should be allowed to make films in which you are murdered. That takes you to a very far point on the issue of freedom of speech.

There's another point that actually took me even longer to come round to and actually it's one of the points on which I've been disagreeing with many of the people working on my behalf at Article 19. It is the question of the law of incitement to murder. Many people were critical of the British government for not prosecuting people in England who made speeches inciting my murder. And frankly, those people included me. I felt on the whole this was wrong and I wished it not to happen.

I think I have just about – I still feel very uneasy about this – come to the position that actually I don't think that I should have felt that I wanted to stop them from saying that. There is a distinction here to be drawn which is the question of whether there is imminent action possible. If I'm standing in the same room as somebody who points at me and tells somebody with a gun or knife that there I am, and I should be killed, that seems to me to be a different thing. That comes under the status of crime. But when people simply stand up on stages around the country, as they did, and say that, in their view, I should be removed from the species, I think probably that's all right.

I still find it very difficult to say that, but I think there is this point about freedom of speech. It has to be the thing you loathe that you tolerate, otherwise you don't believe in freedom of speech.

I want to go on to another aspect of what's been happening about which there's been very little said. It comes back to the point about this not being just a dispute between western ideas about freedom and eastern fascist states, religious states. Because there's a sense in which the case of *The Satanic Verses* is unprecedented – the dimension of international terrorism aimed at a person in another country by order of a mullah.

What's not new is the sense in which this has a context in that it belongs in a category of acts of repression, aimed against writers and thinkers in Muslim countries that has been going on in a very systematic way, not just in Iran, for the last 15 or 20 years. I think you have to understand it as being just one fight in that war.

It's less than 15 years since Saudi Arabia declared a jihad against modernism. The entire form, the entire, enormously rich form of human activity known as the modernist movement, was declared to be un-Islamic and the practitioners of this un-Islamic form were held to be blasphemers and heretics. At this point there followed a fantastic act of persecution against many writers and thinkers in Saudi Arabia, some of whom had their work banned. Others were personally persecuted, some had to go into exile, some were stripped of citizenship. A jihad, a holy war against modernism itself.

Iran, of course, has been killing its writers all the time. One of the reasons why Iran is so surprised about the fuss about *The Satanic Verses* is that they didn't understand why people objected to the idea of killing writers. I mean, that's what you do to writers. It confuses them that people should think otherwise.

Actually, sometimes I suspect that people don't think that much otherwise. They just don't have the conviction to follow through on the idea that writers should be squashed like bugs. Iran, in the same year as *The Satanic Verses* was published, murdered at least ten or eleven of its own writers – to this day they lie in unmarked graves and have no memorial.

It's not only Iran. In a theoretically moderate Muslim country like Egypt one of the most prominent secular thinkers, Faraq Foda, was assassinated by Islamic fundamentalists in the middle of last year. Only two weeks ago the religious seminary which in Egypt has ultimate sanction over matters religious banned all his books posthumously. Meanwhile, writers are having their work raided at the Cairo book fair. One writer, Alaa Hamid, was sentenced last year to an eight-year jail sentence, and so were his publisher and printer.

The sentence is currently suspended while the case is fought out, and one hopes it won't be applied, but the point to remember is that in every case where writers have been persecuted around the Muslim world, the argument against them is identical, word for word, to the attack on *The Satanic Verses*. The argument is always un-Islamic behaviour, offence, insult, blasphemy, heresy, apostacy. This is the language with which inquisitions destroy thought and it is being used throughout the Muslim world right now. It must be fought and one can only say to a European audience: "Remember your history."

What happened is happening again. Arturo Ui says it well at the end of Brecht's play *The Rise and Fall of Arturo Ui*. The actor playing the Hitler character comes to the front of the stage, removes his make-up, and speaks the last line of the play: "The bitch that bore him is in heat again." And I think in the case of the kind of fascistic attacks on thought which were characteristic of the Inquisition, that bitch is in heat again.

Some years ago I wrote an essay called "Is nothing sacred?" to which really the answer is "No". That was the short version of the essay. In that essay I used the image of literature as being a room in a house. If you imagine society as being a house, then in that house there are these little rooms. When you go into these rooms, you hear voices talking to you and those voices talk to you about everything in the world in every possible way. And if you take those rooms away, the people who live in those houses start going crazy. What we need, and if literature is for anything – I resist a utilitarian explanation of literature – it is to be that room in the house where people talk about every possible thing in every possible way.

And the moment you prevent books from being that, you remove not just the freedom of writers, you remove also the freedom of readers. You remove all our freedom to understand our world in the most plural and most diverse form in which it can exist. The attack on *The Satanic Verses* is only one small attack in the much larger fight.

I recall the line of Pablo Neruda, talking about another form of assault, when he said one minute of darkness will not make us blind.

GOVERNMENT AND BUSINESS SECRECY

Michael Mills

Freedom of information is not something to be achieved because it helps journalists, because some of the best journalism is achieved through sheer tenacity and through sheer dedication in following a good story and getting at the truth.

We're very lucky in Ireland that we haven't yet succumbed to the idiot culture, but there are from time to time signs that we might be tending in that direction, because there is always a tendency towards the lowest common denominator. But we have, in fact, in Ireland a very high quality of journalism, on a par with the best in the world. In the past two years – 1991 and 1992 were exceptional years for Irish journalism – the amount of investigative journalism in those years was I think better than ever achieved in the history of newspapers in Ireland.

1991 was a great year. The amount of scandals exposed was quite remarkable and they were exposed only because of the dedication and the tenacity of individual journalists who stayed with the story and refused to be put off; they made us aware for the first time of the extent to which normal standards had declined in many years of business in Ireland.

In this session we will get further insights into the nature of political business secrecy and of the extent to which freedom of information might enable us to become more aware of the things that are happening. People are entitled to know why decisions are being taken by their politicians and by their leading business people, but especially by their politicians, who are being paid by the taxpayer.

Anthony Lewis

I WAS LONDON Correspondent for the *New York Times* for seven years and I'm going to start by talking about different cultural attitudes towards the questions we have before us. Britain has a culture of secrecy which was exemplified to me particularly by two episodes that struck me as very strange, very alien and depressing.

The first was what's come to be known as the Thalidomide Case. The drug Thalidomide, a tranquilliser which was prescribed for pregnant women, turned out to cause grotesque birth defects. Children were born without arms and legs, and when after this event occurred some dozen times, maybe a hundred or more, the drug was stopped and the parents of these children, most of them very modest or poor, sued the distributor of the drug which was of German origin.

The British distributor was Distillers, a very large company that, as I recall, controlled most of the whiskey sales – quite a profitable business in Britain – and the victims sued them for damages. These several suits lay unpressed on the calendar – that is, nobody did anything about them for a period of ten or 12 years. Then the *Sunday Times*, which was then (alas no longer) a hard-hitting investigative newspaper under the editorship of Harry Evans, began a series of articles called "Our Thalidomide Children" describing what had happened to these children and their families, and proposing to conclude with an article about how this dangerous drug had come to be distributed by Distillers.

After two instalments had been printed, Distillers – here we have a combination of business secrecy and government secrecy – persuaded the Attorney General to bring an action to suppress the remaining articles on the ground that they would interfere with the pending lawsuits and hence be in contempt of court. They also argued that the last of the proposed articles about how the drug came to be distributed would be based in part on internal Distillers company documents – documents about tests of the drug before it was distributed – and, hence, would be in violation of a common law doctrine among the most amazing and outrageous in the entire panoply of strange and outrageous British legal doctrines. It's called the Law of Confidence.

Businesses are entitled to suppress violations of their confidence even if they are socially evil, even if the confidence has to do with a drug that caused terrible birth defects. And, sure enough, the British courts granted the injunctions. The *Sunday Times* was prevented from continuing its series of articles and we might never have known what we do know about Thalidomide if the *Sunday Times* had not gone to the expense of bringing an action before the European Commission and then the European Court of Human Rights which, by a very narrow decision, held that the suppression of the articles violated the free speech, free press guarantee in the European Convention on Human Rights.

And the court did a very clever thing. Perhaps lacking full confidence in the rapid execution of its decision – that is, the rapid clearance of the way for publication of the last article about the internal activities of Distillers – it appended to its judgement a copy of the article which enabled everyone to read it at once. It showed that Distillers had very good reason to know, because of tests, that Thalidomide was a dangerous drug but that it distributed it nevertheless.

Then, shortly after that decision, I happened to be at the annual garden party of one of the inns of court in London. I have a great admiration for British lawyers, and some of them are my friends, so I don't mean to be unkind, but at the garden party I was in conversation with the wife of a distinguished lawyer and I expressed my feelings about the Thalidomide case.

She said, "Oh, I think it was terrible."

I asked, thinking she was on my side, "What do you mean?"

And she said, "Oh, to publish those articles. I hate trial by newspaper."

There in a nutshell was the attitude, the cultural secrecy. It's better to have children born deformed, and better to have a system in which you never find out the reasons for this awful event; better to have that, than to have the light of day thrown upon the situation.

I should say it was even worse than I have intimated, because during the ten or 12 years not only was there no freedom for the newspapers to explore the reasons for this tragedy, but those who sought to raise the question in parliament were stopped by the Speaker on the ground that the matter was *sub judice*, another rule in the panoply of British silencing law. The *sub judice* rule means that not even parliament can discuss matters if they are in some ways considered to be before the courts, although these suits were just lying there and with nothing happening to them.

That was one episode in the culture of secrecy that I experienced in London. Another which I'll mention only briefly was the *Crossman Diaries* case, which touches on the very issue that's recently been decided here – the right to disclose what happens inside the cabinet.

Richard Crossman was sort of Peck's bad boy, an American expression that means somebody who, although a leading politician and a member of the Labour cabinet, had a kind of bad boy side to him. He was a great gossip, he loved to argue, and during cabinet meetings while he was in government used to keep a diary. And everyone saw what he was doing, his colleagues all knew that he was keeping this diary because he sat there during these tedious meetings making notes.

In due course, after the Labour government fell – indeed while there was another Labour government – he caused the diaries to be published. He had them prepared for publication and then he died, and his literary executors, who included his widow, Michael Foot, later the leader of the Labour Party, and Graham Greene – not the author but the publisher – caused the diaries to be published. Once again the *Sunday Times* serialised it, and after the second publication in the paper the Attorney General went to court to stop the publication on the ground that they would violate the same Law of Confidence.

I should emphasise that Crossman was the Minister for Housing. He knew nothing whatever about any national security matters. He didn't have a word in the diaries about questions of defence, or foreign policy, or MI5, or anything that you might think had some relation to a need for secrets. But what he did do was to comment freely on the follies of his colleagues, and I guess they didn't like that very much.

In due course the Lord Chief Justice decided the case, and in a wonderfully shrewd way. He said the Law of Confidence does cover cabinet meetings and that the government can get an injunction to stop the publication of cabinet secrets even years after the event. But, he said, I've read this book and it doesn't seem to me worth stopping. In that way he achieved his legal objective, while at the same time putting down the book and hoping to reduce its sales. That was the second episode that, I think, exemplified the culture of secrecy.

Now, of course, I'm an American and it's mainly the experience in my own country that I should talk to you about. I'll take a few minutes to talk about American history. It's a very interesting history, and not as one-sided as you might think. We haven't been a holy land of freedom of information since the year 1788.

I think Carl Bernstein was a little optimistic when he said the First Amendment has been powerful, or has kept us powerfully free from the beginning. It was a long struggle to make the words of the First Amendment mean what they seem to say.

"Congress shall make no law abridging the freedom of speech or of the press." Sounds pretty sweeping but it was not always so read. Right at the beginning, seven years after the first amendment was adopted in 1791, Congress passed a Seditious Libel Act that made it a crime to say impolite things about the President of the United States. It was a device by the political party that then held power, the Federalist Party, to suppress the opposition newspapers in the period running up to the next election, the elections of 1800, and they put a lot of editors in jail. They put an opposition member of Congress in jail for saying that John Adams, the president, was a vain man.

The constitutionality of the law was not tested in the Supreme Court but it was a terrible political failure. The Jeffersonians – Thomas Jefferson was the opposition candidate – used the act to warn against the Federalist Party becoming a tyranny, and a lot of members of the public were persuaded. Jefferson defeated Adams in the election and pardoned all those who had been convicted under the Sedition Act.

I want to read one thing that was said at the time by the author of the First Amendment, a leading constitutional figure, about the Sedition Act, because I really think that it underlies a lot of what we are talking about. James Madison, really the father of our Constitution, in opposing the act said: "It should produce universal alarm because it is levelled against the right of freely examining public characters and measures and of free communication among the people thereon which has ever been justly deemed the only effectual guardian of every other right."

The right of "freely examining public characters and measures". That's really what we're talking about. The right to look into public officials and their policies and businesses in the same way. Madison understood it in somewhat antique language, but I think he got to the root of it right at the beginning, and I want to say that the people in those days, politicians in those days, didn't like newspapers any more than they do today.

You mustn't think that the American politicians who wrote and believed the First Amendment did so because they were enamoured of the press. On the contrary, they thought it was a wretched nuisance. Jefferson is famous for having said, "If I had to choose between a government without newspapers or newspapers without government I would unfailingly choose the latter." But he said that before he was elected president. Afterwards he said a couple of things that are a little more his true views: "I deplore the putrid state into which our newspapers have passed and the malignity, the vulgarity and the mendacious spirit of those who write them. These ordures are rapidly depraving the public taste." A little later he wrote to a friend, "Nothing can now be believed which is seen in a newspaper. Truth itself becomes suspicious by being put into that polluted vehicle."

So it wasn't out of love of the press, it was out of their understanding of how freedom works. If citizens are to be the ultimate sovereigns of a country, they have to be informed of what is happening. They have to know. Otherwise how can they exercise the duty of citizenship? Madison put it in virtually those words.

Well, that's the glorious idea in America, but for a long time it was not observed in fact. During the First World War, those who disagreed with American policy when we entered the war – pacifists, socialists, anarchists – were imprisoned on the thinnest evidence. The most terrible case occurred at the very end of the war when a group of anarchists threw from the tops of buildings in the New York garment district pamphlets opposing President Wilson's decision to send troops to Russia after the Bolshevik revolution.

They were found to be in violation of the Espionage Act for those pathetic pamphlets and had sentences of 20 years in prison imposed on them. The Supreme Court upheld all those convictions despite the First Amendment which seems to say that they have a right to utter their opinions. But there was an important thing. There was a dissent by Justice Holmes, our great free speech judge. I will read a few of his rather amazing words:

Persecution for the expression of opinions seems to me perfectly logical. If you have no doubt of your premises, or your power, and want a certain result with all your heart, you naturally express your wishes in law and sweep away all opposition. But when men have realised that time has upset many fighting faiths, they may come to believe, even more than they believe the very foundations of their own conduct, that the ultimate good desired is better reached by a free trade in ideas, that the best test of truth is the power of the thought to get itself accepted in the competition of the market. That at any rate is the theory of our constitution. It is an experiment, as all life is an experiment. While that experiment is part of our system I think we should be eternally vigilant against attempts to check the expression of opinion that we loathe and believe to be fraught with death.

Not many judgements of that quality are written today. I thought of it last night when Salman Rushdie spoke about how he has learnt the importance of allowing the expression of views that he disagrees with, including those counselling his own death. And he used the word loathe. "I've come to see that I must allow opinions that I loathe." Holmes uses that same word.

Opinions gradually come to be. This doctrine of Holmes, expressed in dissent in 1919, 30 years later came to be accepted by the country. Generally in the United States now it's accepted that you can't stop the expression of loathsome opinions. The Sinn Féin law, Section 31, would be unconstitutional in the United States, without a doubt.

But facts are another matter, and facts are mostly what we're talking about – that is, the right to publish facts that embarrass the government, to get the facts about corruption and bad policy. That was Watergate. That was the Pentagon Papers.

In the case of the Pentagon Papers, the *New York Times* and then the *Washington Post* published secret documents which gave the history of how we got into the Vietnam war, that unfortunate war. The United States government tried to stop it, went to court and, fortunately, failed. The government witnesses said, virtually, that the country would come to an end, the republic would be destroyed if these documents were printed. The North Vietnamese would win immediately and kill all our men. It was complete humbug. The documents were published. Nobody today can remember a word of what they said. Nothing happened. It was the usual case of government exaggeration.

And then came Watergate, Carl Bernstein and Bob Woodward's great achievement. Mr Mills spoke of their determination, their commitment. They had another great advantage. Those two young men had a great advantage in that they were not part of the journalistic establishment. They were young reporters.

The danger in Washington is not so much the culture of secrecy as the culture of intimacy. It's the politicians and the big knobs of the press dining together, drinking together, and being nice to each other, and the press not challenging them. They didn't care about that. There's the famous episode when they called up Henry Kissinger, and Kissinger, in his usual way, rambled on on the telephone. After he'd spoken he said, "Of course, all this is off the record," because that's the basis on which he used to talk to his reporter friends in the press. And they said, "Oh no it's not, we didn't say anything about that." Kissinger spluttered and blew up, but it was too late, and that's why they had their achievement.

I'd like to be able to say that as a result of that the silver cord between the press and government has been cut and the culture of intimacy destroyed. But it's not true. As Carl said last night, the press is not sufficiently challenging in the United States. We have a Freedom of Information Act that works rather well, but we let the government get away with too much still, much too much.

One only has to cite the example of the Iran-Contra affair to know that there is still too much secrecy, and too much latitude for secrecy, and insufficient commitment and energy in the press; because it was a scandalous episode, as bad as Watergate. Worse in a way, I think. The underlying crime was much worse. The crime in Watergate began with the second-rate burglary and became a cover-up and a cover-up of the cover-up. Iran-Contra was something much worse. It was the deliberate violation of the Constitution by the president and his men, and yet it never has been totally exposed and President Bush managed, through his own obfuscation and finally his pardons, to conceal much of what went on.

But I'm not altogether depressed. I think there is something about our country that is not a culture of secrecy. It's a culture in which, in the end, most things do come out. I'd like to end by reading one more passage from a Supreme Court opinion. It was the opinion of Justice Black, our greatest First Amendment advocate in modern times, in the Pentagon Papers case. Remember the *Times* and the *Post*, and then other papers had published the secrets of the origin of the Vietnam war and the government had tried to stop it.

Here's Justice Black:

The press was protected in the First Amendment so that it could bare the secrets of government and inform the people. Only a free and unrestrained press can effectively expose deception in government, and paramount among the responsibilities of a free press is the duty to prevent any part of the government from deceiving the people and sending them off to distant lands to die of foreign fevers and foreign shot and shell. In my view, far from deserving the condemnation of their courageous reporting, the *New York Times*, the *Washington Post*, and other newspapers should be commended for serving the purpose of the founding fathers all so clearly. In revealing the workings of government that led to the Vietnam war the newspapers notably did precisely that which the founders hoped and trusted they would do.

Dr Garret FitzGerald

I'M GOING LARGELY to follow Anthony Lewis in basing my remarks on my own experience. I have to say that the issue of freedom of information is one which I have not fully or adequately considered. My heart is in the right place, but my head is still not totally clear as to where exactly the line should be drawn. I would greatly enjoy a full discussion and debate in this country on this subject. It would enable us to improve radically on the present situation. But it is not a subject I have given sufficient consideration to, and so I reserve the right to contradict myself subsequently if convinced things are different.

As has been said, I have been a bit of a journalist of sorts all my life. I never secured enough of my livelihood from it to be allowed to join the union, but it has been a source of supplementary income except, unhappily, when in government when you're precluded from it. And, because I was involved in journalism long before I was in politics, I never came to share this most noticeable characteristic of politicians, paranoia about the press. It's always entertained me greatly.

I have to admit to having been occasionally irritated by press reports, but only one really got under my skin in all those years. It was a report in the *Sunday World* headlined "Garret's Mum Spent £104 on Cosmetics". My mother was 25 years dead, was a Victorian in her origins and in much of her demeanour and behaviour, and to my knowledge never spent more than half a crown a year on powder. It seems to me an allegation which could perhaps have been omitted and was totally invented.

Now, apart from occasions like that, I haven't really been much bothered about the press and my sympathies have tended to lie with them even when they have been having a go at my own administration. That said, this is a complex issue. There is a powerful prima facie case, of course, for minimising secrecy, but also, in order to make things work with reasonable efficiency, to be able to keep some things private both in business and in government, at least for some period of time.

So in this matter we face an inherent conflict between two rights in both senses of the word, right. And the conflict is necessarily difficult to resolve because the people who have to resolve it are governments who are strongly *parti pris* on one side of the issue, and will be slow to move because of their own, we'll call it vested interest, or at least instinctive tendency to preserve the status quo. The other problem is the fact that the issues involved are multifarious and complex and do need to be teased out in detail in ways that nobody has attempted yet.

I would add one other point with Anthony Lewis here from the United States: I think one also has to make the point that there are cultural differences between countries. Not just in the extremes of Britain on the one hand and the United States and Scandinavia on the other, but over the spectrum. To give you an example: I personally have no difficulty about the idea of the state publishing people's tax returns and what they earn. It seems to make life much simpler, and also more interesting for us all, of course.

But if that were proposed here, as is done in other countries – I've seen lists of what people earn in America, published in tax returns, and in Scandinavia – there would be a howl of protest, not just from government, but from people. We have a great sense of privacy about our own affairs, and I think the Irish popular, or public culture is not as libertarian in this matter as it is in other countries. There are areas where government cannot go beyond the democratic consensus. So I suspect that, with the best will in the world, if we move towards freedom of information, public opinion will not allow us to go as far as perhaps other countries would.

That reference to tax reminds me of the National Archives which I had the pleasure of getting going through introducing a bill – the only bill I actually introduced as Taoiseach. (When it was opened by my successor in office, I went along to the opening. The draft speech given to the Taoiseach contained no references to me, but by looking him straight in the eye as he spoke, I morally forced him to put in a paragraph of his own giving me the necessary credit, which he did, I must say.) I had a look at the indexes that were up at the side behind the desk. I looked at the Foreign Affairs index and went back as far as I could, to the founding of the state, and there was a file: – Frank FitzGerald Restricted. He was my uncle. Now I know my uncle sold arms to Michael Collins who had some idea of invading the North and who didn't want to use the guns the British were giving him to deal with the republicans for that purpose. So he got the arms from my uncle, and it was a very devious transaction, disowned by the Public Accounts Committee afterwards. My uncle was felt not to have given sufficient value for money, and there were a lot of problems. But all that's in the public forum.

What on earth was the file restricted for? So I asked our friend in charge of Foreign Affairs about this. He said he'd have another look. He'd had to do it rather hastily and perhaps some things had been restricted rather hastily and unnecessarily... And he did restrict it, and do you know why? Because the question of the tax payable by my uncle on the profits of the arms transaction were dealt with in the file. It was the tax that was the problem, not the arms importation. Which makes my point about tax.

That said, any standard in the area of government secrecy extends far more widely than is necessary and the thrust should clearly be towards greater openness. And this was brought home to me when I was writing my autobiography because I faced the question of what I should not say – my instinct is to say as much as possible.

There are certain restraints I imposed for myself. I wouldn't want to hurt people – that's a personal limitation, nothing to do with government secrecy. Obviously there are security implications, and public security I wouldn't refer to, but, after that, I couldn't really see what I couldn't say. And the more I wrote the less reason I saw to withhold anything. I therefore gave a full detailed account of things between the Anglo-Irish negotiators and this didn't disturb anyone, even when I made a number of references to the British Intelligence interception of messages from the Irish Embassy in London to us. That was thought a matter so trivial that nobody bothered to mention it in a review and there were many reviews of the book.

So I was quite right in thinking that there was no reason to withhold anything and the over-caution that people expressed is really not warranted.

I did, however, avoid saying anything about who said what, and there were two reasons for this. One, a feeling that there is an argument for caution here because otherwise you will inhibit subsequent ministers from giving their views. I know from talking to ministers who were worried about what I put in the book that it did worry people who might be in government again, of several parties – and might have an adverse affect on subsequent government discussions. And I didn't put that in, but another good reason is that my memory is very poor anyway for repetitive meetings, and what happened at what meeting, and if I said that somebody said something I would almost certainly be wrong. But even if I had the records, I would have been doubtful about it.

I did, however, in one instance give the vote in a cabinet discussion where it seemed to me necessary for the reader to understand the nature of the story and what was happening. That was the vote of 14 to two against my initial proposal to have a New Ireland Forum.

But I did limit myself in that respect. Otherwise I didn't see any reason to, and I think there is far too much emphasis on secrecy when there isn't a reason for it.

I should now say something about the Irish method of dealing with ministerial documents. It is quite different from the position in Britain. From the early period, from 1924 onwards, ministers leaving office certainly took their private papers with them – that is, the papers of their private office. These form the basis of collections of papers, most of which are in the UCD archives, including the Mulcahy papers, the McGilligan papers, my father's papers which I put in there. And, indeed, these were used by historians before they were released from 1973 onwards when Liam Cosgrave decided to release papers.

That practice continued. Indeed my father took with him 12 tin boxes and a large cardboard box. I have, I think, 460 boxes. The tin boxes proved very useful because I inherited a couch from my parents and, at a certain point, three legs had fallen off and it was supported by three boxes of state papers. When I handed my father's papers over to the archives, we had to buy a new couch.

But that practice exists. I don't think in Britain, as I understand it, that it happens in the same way. Ministers are supposed to have to go to the cabinet office to consult papers before writing anything. It's a bit laborious.

The situation has not been abused in this country as far as I am aware. Ministers have stored these papers, and current papers would not be made accessible in ways that would be undesirable. There is no reason, I think, to change this practice of allowing ministers to take papers, but in 1977 when the government came to an end all the desks in my office were piled high with boxes of the papers I was taking. They were going to the UCD archives – in those days behind my Iveagh House desk in the room next door where Dudley Edwards and the UCD archives lived.

Unfortunately, we couldn't make a hole in the chimney, so we had to go down the stairs and up again to go into the archives. There were boxes piled everywhere and my private secretary said, "Minister, I have to tell you this. We were told there is a cabinet ruling you can't take any papers with you."

I said, "What?"

He said, "Don't mind, it's all right. Don't worry about it. You just ask why this is the case, and the Taoiseach will say because of Section 3, I think it is; Section something of the Official Secrets Act. You will then say, 'Taoiseach, ah yes, but if you take that in conjunction with Section 2, and sub section 56.6, surely this is not the case,' and I think you'll be all right."

So I went through this procedure. The only difference was the cabinet secretary was put up and pressed to answer the questions. And when we pressed him as to why we couldn't take the papers he had an extraordinary theory that it was because the ruling referred to former ministers retaining documents. He said that if you were a former minister you couldn't retain something, because by the time you're "former", it wouldn't be retention. If you retained it, you're a minister, therefore this can't happen. The cabinet burst out laughing.

We all ignored the injunction and I'm sure the cabinet minutes, I never actually saw them of course, recorded the decision that we should not have taken the papers. And that has never been an inhibition here. Nor do you have to go to the cabinet secretary when you're publishing your memoirs, as in Britain. The reason for this difference is, curiously, not a difference in cabinet practice, I believe, but because in Britain, when you become a member of the cabinet, if you're not already a privy councillor, you become one and you swear a privy councillor's oath of secrecy. That's where the problem comes from.

I think our practice is sensible and it hasn't given rise to any difficulty. There is in the Official Secrets Act a right of the Taoiseach to ask you for the papers back. And that seems reasonable because you might take the only copy.

And the issue doesn't pose the kind of problems it does in Great Britain, partly because we're more sensible here. I think I can recall a British cabinet minister, and I may be wrong about this – this is one of the things I'm never quite certain if I dreamt it or if it happened so don't take me too literally – telling me over the Strasbourg case (we were accusing the British of torture), that the Labour government had difficulty in defending it because they were not allowed to see the papers of their predecessors. Perhaps that's not true, but I think I was told that. It's actually quite a mad way to run a government.

Mind you, there are possible abuses here. It has happened here – and I believe the first person to do it was Conor Cruise O'Brien – that a minister uses the papers of the previous administration to embarrass his predecessor by citing him. It's happened a few times here, and it's an objectionable practice. It requires a strong convention against abuse, which I think could be introduced here without difficulty. The number of cases of abuse has been limited.

On the one occasion that I looked for the papers of my predecessor, it was in relation to the negotiations with the British. I did ask to see the papers relating to the negotiations between my predecessor and Margaret Thatcher as I was taking up from there, and I had to know what had happened. But I've been careful not to use these subsequently in any way in my autobiography and to exclude them from my mind in writing my autobiography because it would be improper.

But to have a rule that you cannot see the papers in any circumstances, I think, is an unnecessary inhibition on government. Common sense and reasonable convention should prevail.

Now, moving back from the historical to the contemporary, there are problems that can arise if government discussions are leaked, particularly at the time they are taking place. It can have security implications and I'll give you a good example of that: we were told on a Wednesday that £2 million of IRA funds were in a bank in Meath, and we had to legislate in such a way that both houses would meet and pass a Bill after half-past three the following Tuesday, and have it signed by the President that night so that the money could be seized before the banks opened the next day.

We managed to come through that six days making 21 drafts of the bill to try and get its constitutionality right. Seizing property is difficult in this country because the law is in favour of property. And it didn't get out. It was very important it didn't. Had it leaked out, obviously, it would have been very damaging to the country. That's a clear case where cabinet secrecy at the time is of vital importance.

But it is also important, not merely in relation to the budget, but in relation to other decisions government may take where the knowledge of the impending decision may enable somebody to make a profit or to take advantage of it personally. Or, and this is a less clear-cut case but, I believe, an important one, where it would enable a vested interest to start a lobby against something being done which might prevent or inhibit a desirable action, because vested interests are very powerful when they get going in any democratic political system.

These are cases where, I think, in the short-run, government secrecy can be important. One has to accept that there are such cases. The difficulty lies in the area between the short-run of protection of what's actually happening at the time, and the long-run disclosure which isn't a great problem. It's the intermediate area which is the difficult one, and that's the area which I have not given enough thought to. I would like to hear much more about other countries' practice.

I have been told by a senior American official – and he may not be correct – that the American Freedom of Information Act has had the effect that much of government goes on either orally, or, if there are documents, documents do not find their way into government papers. All that has happened has been to push things more underground, he claims.

Now, I don't know whether it's true or not and, obviously, the senior official who told me this had an interest in convincing me of it because it suited his cause against too much freedom of information. But, nonetheless, it is a possible danger one has to guard against, and, therefore, where you draw the line and what provisions you have are matters that do need careful consideration.

In all this there is the distinction between the public interest and the political interest. Naturally politicians like to think that all their interests are in the public interest. Many of them are purely political protection of themselves. It cannot be left totally to politicians to decide for themselves, as they would abuse it, but how do you control it without undermining the appropriate degree of secrecy which is necessary for the carrying on of government business, at least in the short term.

I think there is one area in this country that we need to look at, and it's come up very recently. It is the question of replies to parliamentary questions. The practice here has been of minimum disclosure. The draft furnished by a civil servant to a minister is one written on the basis that the civil servant's primary duty is to protect his minister from possible political attack. Therefore, "say the minimum","disclose the least possible". The mnister then has to add in the information he thinks should be given.

Now, I think there should be a code of conduct under which civil servants' primary duty is to the public interest, not loyalty to the minister. I've always thought this. I thought it long before I went into politics and I still think it. There is a problem here. It's understandable. It is that the civil servants can transfer their loyalty from one administration to the next, which is a very good thing – much better than the American system of thousands of people being pushed in and out all the time.

But it is carried too far. And I think some kind of duty on civil servants to the public interest primarily, and only secondly to the minister, needs to be imposed – and civil servants take those codes of conduct very seriously. Something can be done here.

There's one danger in this, of course. That if you do that, and leave it to the minister to suppress rather than the civil servant in the original draft answer, the minister may suppress, may mislead. The civil service replies will always be designed not to tell an untruth but to hide the truth, but the minister might actually mislead himself into telling an untruth.

Perhaps the civil servant should have a right to look at the final reply and require that at least it isn't telling an untruth. That is perhaps all too complex. But certainly the problem of inadequate replies to parliamentary questions and acceptance of a degree of disclosure and of quite brutal non-disclosure, a refusal to discuss the matter, is a very bad feature of our system.

Of course it was indicted by Justice Hamilton in the Beef Tribunal. He, I think, made the point that the tribunal might not have been needed if adequate replies had been given in the first instance. And the opposition somehow has not been able to secure the degree of disclosure, and the degree of sense of responsibility of disclosure, that is desirable. But there are two separate issues here.

One is the answer which avoids the question, the answer which answers a different question: that's a matter for the opposition to note the evasion and immediately to pick it up. I read every parliamentary answer to see in what way it differed from the question, and one could see immediately what the truth was. I have to say that very often politicians in opposition are not quick enough or astute enough to see the evasion at the time, and the press never seem to notice it. I'd have a man watching every one of these evasions and there would be a column in the paper each day to deal with it.

There is, secondly, an increasing tendency to refuse to answer the question at all – lump questions together, answer two of them, don't answer the others, and get away with it. But that should not be allowed. Lumping questions together may be desirable, but there should be a requirement that some answer be given to each question.

The last thing I want to talk about is journalism. We have a need in this country to change the whole climate in the area of possible government abuses. I have for many years been deeply frustrated by the existence of a climate in which anyone who suggests there may be an abuse of power is immediately stigmatised as "self-righteous" – a dreadful word of abuse in Ireland, far worse than saying you're a murderer. To have it said you're self-righteous kills you completely, and it was used against me for years – and, I have to say, in my own party the pressure was on me. "Really it's not a good thing to raise all these issues, you'll be very unpopular...." Any suggestion of abuse by government tends to be frowned on as if it's a disgraceful thing to do or say.

And the press has gone along with this. Let me just give one example. Let me tell you why we have all the scandals that Michael Mills referred to. The reason is that one journalist managed to bring out the Greencore scandal. What happened then? A whole lot of other things came out. All of those were known as allegations beforehand, but had never been published anywhere, not alleged in the Dáil by an opposition intimidated by these charges of righteousness, and not put forward by journalists. But once the dam broke, it all flooded out.

Why hadn't it come out before? I'll give you a case. One of the issues raised – I won't go into the merits of the issues – is the Kinsealy drainage case. It was raised in the Dáil by Nora Owen very effectively in a series of questions before all these issues came out in the papers, before there was a big row with Kinsealy later on.

What happened? A number of the papers didn't publish it at all. And, as far as I know, only one did. And what they published was a tiny little paragraph of about two sentences, because it was embarrassing. Allegations against the Taoiseach? You couldn't put that into the paper. That was the atmosphere, the climate. I think that was not good journalism.

It's no good just blaming politicians. OK, we're at fault. We were all too easily intimidated by this atmosphere, but that attitude was helped by the press because, I can tell you, if you raised matters you could be attacked in the press for irresponsibility in making allegations for which "there's really no foundation", and for lowering the tone of politics. That's the atmosphere in the press and in the parliament. And that's why we have these scandals.

They wouldn't have accumulated to that point if we'd been dealing with them year by year, as time went on. And that blame is widely shared. Now that we have a new climate, I hope that we will have a more vigilant press and more vigilant parliament in future.

And I have one more point to make. If we are going to have a public broadcasting system which is going to be as open as it should be, we need to ensure that it is under an authority which is not appointed by methods that result in the members of staff feeling under pressure.

I only appointed one RTE Authority. I was asked beforehand in the Dáil if we were going to make political appointments, and I made it clear that I was going to reappoint one person who was close to our party and I would make no other political appointments. And I did that. When we came to discuss it in government, I said, "Look, we want to get an Authority, we want to get people who will stand up to any government, us or the next. Who will we get?" And we had a long discussion around the cabinet table trying to think of the people whose integrity and dedication was such that if we put them in there they wouldn't be intimidated by anyone, including ourselves. I'm not sure if other Authorities were appointed on that basis. And I don't think you can rely on governments to do it all the time.

But perhaps the appointments should be made by some other

system. Leaving it purely to a political government can lead to appointments being made which do have a negative effect on the view within RTE of where their duty lies. I'm not saying that they should necessarily act like the *Sunday Business Post* or the *Tribune,* but they shouldn't be as inhibited about reporting what's in the papers as they have been.

And finally there are changes in relation to *sub judice* in the Dáil that I hope are going to be be made. This very week we have seen Mr O'Malley repeatedly ordered by the Ceann Comhairle, on the grounds of *sub judice,* not to proceed further because he was explaining what had happened in the case of the alleged purloined documents or photocopied documents. This was ludicrous. You can go out to the street outside and make a statement and there's no problem, but you can't say it in the Dáil. The *sub judice* rule has to be changed, and I hope it will be changed.

Mary Raftery

ANY JOURNALIST WHO has worked in the area of investigating business, investigating fraud, investigating wrongdoing, knows clearly that business in this country operates behind a very effective and fully functioning cloak of secrecy.

Virtually all the doors are firmly closed against anybody who is seeking even the most basic information on commercial activities. There is a myriad of perfectly legal ways that exist to allow companies to hide from public view the assets at their disposal, the deals they engage in, and even who owns those particular companies. That no serious attempt has been made by the authorities to breach that impenetrable veil of secrecy has, I believe, two very serious consequences for us and for our system in this country. Firstly, it makes breaking the fraud laws, the few fraud laws that we have, much easier than it might otherwise be. I'll return to that point later, but, secondly, it creates a huge degree of public distrust of a major sector of the Irish economy.

During the height of the spate of scandals that have been referred to here, just over a year ago, I commissioned a major study of public opinion for a *Today Tonight* programme that dealt with the climate of secrecy and with the effects of so many scandals breaking on Irish public opinion. We did expect that there would be some increase in dissatisfaction with business people, with politicians, but, quite frankly, I was taken aback by the scale of the distrust expressed in the survey.

Nine people out of every ten said that there was a golden circle of people who used power for their own personal gain. Eighty-one per cent, four out of five, said that that golden circle was made up equally of business people and politicians. And a similar number, 83 per cent, said that the scandals revealed so far in connection with Greencore, with Telecom's purchase of a site in Ballsbridge, and with the Beef Tribunal, were only the tip of the iceberg, that, in fact, there remained an enormous amount more that was simply being hidden from the people of this country and was not being revealed.

That a huge majority of people would hold those views has really serious implications for our political and our economic system, and I think it makes it imperative to address the secret way in which business is allowed to operate because this, I believe, is the key to the root of that distrust which is indeed well-founded.

One of the main arguments against a more open system of businesses is that companies would be damaged by revealing information to their competitors, and there is obviously a balance to be struck here. But it seems clear to me that if people hold the views expressed in that survey, then the secret nature of the system is in fact doing untold damage to the very sector, the business community, that it is designed to protect. To put it bluntly, if the vast majority of people in the country suspect that most business people are crooks then business has a really serious problem on its hands. Now, I don't particularly believe that most business people are crooks, but I do believe that it is now not only in the public interest, as it has always been, but strongly in the interest of the commercial sector itself to become more open to public scrutiny.

To turn to the area of fraud: it's frequently the case that secrecy in business operates as a very efficient smokescreen to hide criminal activity, and anyone who has attempted to investigate fraud in this country knows just how nightmarishly difficult it can become. It just appears that every conceivable obstacle is being put in your way and in the way of getting at the truth. And the most difficult part of it all to deal with is that most of these obstacles are fully legal. So it's against the law to commit fraud but it's perfectly possible to use fully legal means to cover up fraud or other questionable practices.

I've had particular experience in terms of investigating one case involving questionable practices over a period of nearly ten years. It's the case, which is at this stage fairly notorious, of Patrick Gallagher and the Gallagher group of companies. It pre-dated the recent spate of scandals by a year or 18 months.

I began investigating the huge Gallagher conglomerate in 1982 when Gallagher was essentially buying and selling so much property in Dublin that really he was just playing Monopoly with the streets of the city. At that stage there was no hint of any wrongdoing in the company, but it was still almost impossible to discover what exactly the group owned, what it was buying, what it was selling, and what was the extent of the way it was playing with the streets in the city.

What few regulations which there were on disclosure, and this is still the case, were clearly not being enforced. The files in the Companies Office were out of date and they didn't even give the paltry amount of information they are supposed to give. When the Gallagher group went bust that same year, in 1982, it came as a complete surprise to everyone, a bolt from the blue; the secret way in which Gallagher had been permitted to operate gave no hint and no warning of that collapse. And it was probably particularly acute in that case, because the Gallagher group was so big that the collapse played a not insubstantial part in precipitating the country into the recession of the early '80s.

In fact, so well hidden were Gallagher's difficulties that a mere few months before the collapse the media, particularly the business media, were lionising Gallagher as the man with the Midas touch. He was a brilliant whizz kid who could do no wrong. As some kind of counterpoint to this, the issue of *In Dublin* magazine for which I wrote a long and critical article on Gallagher's business had a memorable title emblazoned in huge bold print on the cover: "Patrick Gallagher, Property Speculator and Brat".

Gallagher refused to be interviewed by me for the article but he organised to meet me afterwards, and the main reason for this was that he seemed very keen to set the record straight and pointed out vociferously that he was not in fact a brat. He wanted everyone to know that he was a committed socialist!

However, to come back to the central point, what I want to make clear is a point about control of information which people spoke about yesterday evening. They talked about information empowering people, and I think the critical point here is obviously who controls that information. In the case of business, the control of that information at the moment in this country rests exclusively in the hands of the business community itself, and they are the ones empowered by this information. They use it as a weapon in their quest for profit and they make public only what is to their advantage and at the times that suit them. Gallagher, for instance, was well known for releasing information to his advantage, about huge profits he'd made on property transactions at times when this was very useful to him in terms of other deals, and he is by no means unique in that. The point about all of this is the media laps it up. It's the only information available to the media and so it's printed and it's broadcast. What we have done as a society is to hand over control of that information about business to the business community itself and, in the absence of the opportunity to get access independently to information the media, in effect, colludes in this abuse of information. At the time that Gallagher was being praised to the skies he was in fact breaking the law. He committed numerous offences under the Companies Act and he was later convicted of fraud in connection with his bank in the North.

Six hundred depositors in his bank in the South lost all their savings because Gallagher was illegally using money which they had deposited in his bank to fund his property speculation and to destroy large tracts of the city into the bargain. It took eight years for that matter to become public.

In 1990 I made a programme for *Today Tonight* revealing the contents of the report of the liquidator into the Gallagher Bank. Up to then the report had remained secret. It contained information of the most serious public interest, which indicated not only serious breaches of the law, but also the inadequacy of those laws, and the fact that they were not being enforced. There is no public right of access to such liquidator's reports, even when there is strong suspicion in the public domain of wrongdoing.

The way we obtained that report was by using the good offices of a creditor of the bank who was entitled to get the report through the court. It was a very long and complicated process and various obstacles were put in our way, but eventually we got the report. After the programme was transmitted there was uproar in the Dáil. Politicians demanding why after all these years, eight years later, Gallagher had not been prosecuted for all of the offences which we detailed in the programme. They were calling, God help us, for all sorts of public inquiries, tribunals and the like. However, we were spared that. At that stage, Gallagher had actually been found guilty of fraud in Northern Ireland, but he had not been charged south of the border. There was no answer given in the Dáil as to why he had not been prosecuted.

Some months after the transmission of the programme, the DPP indicated that no charges would be preferred against Gallagher in the Republic. The DPP, of course, is not required to, and in most cases cannot, give his reasons for instituting or not instituting a prosecution.

In the context of discussing business scandals and malpractice, I think the draconian laws of libel in Ireland become relevant to the area of business. It's not really possible to talk about business coverage and business investigation without dealing in some way with libel. And our own particular experience in the case of Gallagher was really quite serious. Gallagher had well-known political connections to Fianna Fáil which was, at the time we were making the programme, in government, and a senior Fianna Fáil politician appeared in the liquidator's report as having been lent sums of money from Gallagher's bank. He had paid back the money when the liquidator asked him to do so and there wasn't any hint of any wrongdoing on his part: we proposed to say exactly that in the programme. But we were prevented from doing so. Our legal advice was that any mention of the politician's business relationship with Gallagher, in the context of the programme which dealt with the fraud, was potentially libelous. And there were clear indications that the politician was going to sue all round him if we mentioned his loans, despite the fact that there was nothing to suggest that there had been any impropriety or wrongdoing on his part.

It's this kind of enforcement of secrecy that fuels public suspicion, sometimes in ways that are actually totally groundless. It eats away at public confidence in the institutions of the state and in the people who run the country, and that, ultimately, damages our democratic system.

There is another point in relation to that particular programme on Patrick Gallagher. A day or two before its transmission, we received a letter from the Director of Public Prosecutions advising us not to broadcast the programme because it might be in contempt of court if charges were brought at some future date against Gallagher.

A few hours before the transmission of the Gallagher programme, it was pulled as a result of this communication from the DPP. However, mercifully, it was merely a delay. RTE essentially gave indications to the DPP: "All right, we'll give you time to take your charges. We don't want to prejudice any trial and if you don't do it within a certain amount of time we'll put out the programme." The charges were never brought and the programme was transmitted.

In the context of libel, once again, in terms of the programme, we were under what you could only describe as farcical constraints in terms of making a programme on Gallagher. For instance, our legal people would not allow us to say that Patrick Gallagher owned the Gallagher Group of companies, nor in the programme did we ever say who owned the Gallagher Group of companies. And the reason for this is that nobody knows who owns those companies because nobody could find out. It's secret. And this is one of the cornerstones of the mechanisms which companies use to hide their affairs. Gallagher's companies traced their owner-ships to a whole maze of different companies, but all of them ended up being owned by a company called Bearing Estates Ltd, registered in the Cayman Islands.

Now the main reason you would register your parent company in the Cayman Islands is that you have something to hide. Places like the Cayman Island and a myriad of others refuse to reveal de-tails on the directorships and the ownerships of the companies reg-istered in their countries. And this procedure is common in Ireland. If you combine that with the practice of having nominee shareholders – effectively the same procedure, except it's based here – it's one of the most effective, fully legal ways of hiding your business from the public eye and it's this practice which, of course, is at the root of a lot of the current scandals that we are dealing with.

The other aspect of all this is the access of the authorities to in-formation on private businesses. The Revenue Commissioners, and indeed any other relevant government department, have great dif-ficulty in obtaining information on nominee shareholders or on company bank or building society accounts. Their only option, generally, is to obtain a court order, giving them access to such in-formation. But in order to get the court order they must first pre-sent some kind of prima facie evidence of tax evasion or other wrongdoing. It is a classic Catch 22. How can they present the evi-dence if they don't have access to the information in the first place? So it's no wonder that there have been so few cases of fraud or tax evasion brought before our courts.

There are clear areas here which require only the political will to implement changes in the law to make openness and transparency a prerequisite of business activity in this country. The commitment in the new Programme for Government to force political parties publicly to reveal the sources of their funding from business is an indication that perhaps, for the first time in this country, the polit-ical will might now exist.

Finally, I think it's important just to make one or two other points about the area of libel in the consideration of secrecy in the business world. The libel laws in Ireland are an intrinsic part of the arsenal at the disposal of business to prevent investigation and public disclosure of information. They make investigation by journalists of fraud a very hazardous activity, with the result that revelations of criminal business activities are relatively rare in this country despite our recent experience.

This is all the more serious because the Irish fraud laws themselves are hopelessly inadequate and the Garda fraud squad, while very willing, is simply not sufficiently resourced to do the job of detecting and prosecuting business fraud. And with weak fraud laws, with little enforcement of them, and vicious libel laws, Ireland is, in the words of one legal expert from the North, simply a "fraudster's paradise".

There are usually several suspected frauds kicking around journalistic circles at any one time. But in order to publish them, a full court standard of proof is required. Yet this is without any of the powers at your disposal were it to be a real court case, such as disclosure of documents, and so forth. Now, I'm not for an instant advocating at all that unproven allegations should be allowed to be published. There's absolutely no question of that. But what I am saying is that in a libel case, public interest is simply not a defence which carries any real weight at all. The balance is far too heavily weighted at the moment against the public right to know, and in favour of the privacy or the right to secrecy of individuals or companies. It's for this reason that the risks involved to publishers in investigating and printing or broadcasting fraud stories are very high. Because of the difficulties involved, such investigations require a huge investment of time and money, and this is particularly so in the high-profile, high-impact medium of television.

But to television, funded directly by the taxpayer through the licence fee, such programmes revealing frauds are the very essence of what constitutes a public service. I think that it is to our shame, all of us in this country, that it was not our own media that broke the Goodman story and broke the logjam to allow the tribunal to be set up. I and many other journalists within RTE are arguing, and argue all the time, that the necessary investment to investigate fraud is worth making and the necessary risks are worth taking. But, so far, I'm afraid that is a battle that I think we are losing. And I can only hope for the sake of our democracy that in other branches of the media someone else is winning that battle, for the time and for the money to shine the light on business fraud in this country.

John Tierney

I THINK WE have to put in context, before I say anything about our right to information, what the trade union movement is. Essentially, we represent 60 per cent of the workforce in this country, and – contrary to some media reports where we are just seen during disputes as holding the country to ransom – we are a very large social organisation affecting the lives of workers and their families. I think the image that we may have sometimes is partly our own making in not projecting ourselves properly. But we do become involved in things like pension schemes, health and safety, and matters like that which affect people directly, and their families.

In relation to information, there is a general consensus, and has been for decades in this country, that co-operation between the government, the employers, and the trade unions is desirable in the national interest, and over the last five years you will have all seen two very specific national agreements – the Programme for National Recovery and currently the Programme for Economic and Social Progress – where detailed information, targets and agreements were made to turn this economy around and create more jobs.

Our union has been particularly critical of the private sector's role in these agreements, and we believe that they haven't fulfilled or lived up to what they were committed to. Despite this consensus, discussion, openness and communication do not translate themselves into the private sector at all. There are some levels of communication, but in relation to detailed plans, future developments, they don't really exist. We're told a certain amount, and sometimes we've to force certain things.

But we do represent a large social grouping. We have the right to know what is going to happen to our future. We've seen the dramatic closure of some of our companies. Most workers do not do things to jeopardise their future or their company, but, at the end of the day, companies do jeopardise workers' lives, particularly the substantial transnational companies. However, that is the Irish experience as it stands at the moment.

We are now part of the European Community and there are

some models worth looking at in Europe, and two countries in particular. One is Germany where, since the '50s, they have in place what are called works councils, with the right to information and consultation depending on the size of company. In a small company there are certain limitations on what information you can get, but in large companies there is an entitlement to a sub-board structure which meets and explains and informs workers of ongoing developments. These councils have control of certain working conditions, but there is a general consensus in arriving at certain target options and things like that.

The second case is that of France. After the war the French government brought in legislation to protect workers' rights. Every company, once it reaches a certain size, must have a works council, regardless of whether there's a trade union in the company or not. That works council has the right to request information from the managing director, and, in certain circumstances, if that information is not supplied, there are heavy penalties on him personally, including fines, and even, potentially, a jail sentence.

In Ireland our only experience in this matter is worker directors in state enterprises. It's been reasonably successful but needs to be developed, but there is nothing whatsoever in the private sector.

The EC has produced a draft directive called the "The Employee Information and Consultation Directive". It calls for works councils to be created at community-scale undertakings – companies with a thousand employees and at least one hundred employees in two European countries. It is an important document because it does give the workers rights to information about mergers, relocations and things like that, to determine and become part of what is going on and influence the companies' thinking in relation to jobs and rationalisation, if that has to take place, or indeed, if the company is in profitability, its expansion, and to share in that development with the company. In Ireland it's an aspiration. There's a consensus but it doesn't translate itself into action. In the current document, the Programme for Economic and Social Progress, there was a paragraph calling for the Federation of Irish Employers (now called IBEC) and the ICTU to produce guidelines for the private sector for employee participation. That was done, but only as far as a very bland aspirational document, and it's only a strictly voluntary guideline, although it does actually agree that there should be effective development of the enterprise, the need

to maximise competitiveness, increase job satisfaction, closer identification of employees with the organisation and a safe and
healthy working environment. It's clear that the direction of the
document is to improve efficiency and profitability; nothing about
putting workers' representatives on the board; nothing about the
workers' rights to have information directly from the board or
from the owner of the company. There is nothing that gives us the
financial situation, the investment decisions, the change in economic or market environment in which the company operates at
all.

And, once again, there is this resistance, this "yes, we'll tell you
information", but the thing about information, or wanting to
know information, is not the right to ask the question and have it
answered, it's to ask the right question and have it answered.

However, it is also notable that this aspiration has appeared
again in the Programme for Government of our current Fianna
Fáil/Labour coalition where they actually say, "We will encourage
greater co-operation between employers and employees at enterprise level to complement co-operation between employers and
trade unions at national level." They go on to talk about improving equality legislation, conditions of employment and other
EC directives, but I know from the large transnational companies
we deal with that that will not happen unless the trade union
movement itself forces the situation.

Now, in Ireland, there is the constitutional right to join a trade
union, but it's very important to understand the legal positions of
unions in companies. That's fine if you can join the union and
there's legislation to licence trade unions to negotiate. But there is
no law in this country to require any employer to deal with a
union or to allow a union to represent his working staff whatsoever.

And it's not only that the legislation is not there. Employers,
particularly in Europe, and, closer to home, in the UK, already try
to bypass unions in companies that are organised by introducing
what is known as human resource management, which totally indi-
vidualises the situation – and there are some attempts here too.
They deal with the individual on his own, they introduce contracts
to the staff which are renewed every two years. They take away
the collective approach, the influence approach, and the protection approach, that the trade unions have for their members. And

we've also seen in the UK growing derecognition of trade unions.

Now, that has a lot to do with the political climate of that country and I do agree with Garret FitzGerald that there are cultural differences in each country about how they do their business. I believe we have a relatively sophisticated trade union and industrial relations set-up in this country compared to the UK. However, at the end of the day, you end up with a situation where although a trade union can ask for information, they have no way of evaluating that information because it is never comprehensive.

And at the end of the day, we also know that companies, as we are seeing at the moment, do cut back, do affect the economy of a town or a village, they do affect families. Most people will recognise that if there are difficulties then you cut your cloth. We've always functioned on the basis of a company's ability to pay or do something. But there is a reluctance by most employers to give any quality information to us. And it's been my personal experience that in companies that do attempt to try and communicate or give an understanding to staff, there is a healthier relationship. In companies where there is an adversarial role, you then find very damaging disputes or you find very damaging relations, and things are difficult to turn round or change when the company wants to change these things.

I think it's also important to take note of the 1990 Industrial Relations Act. It was brought in to protect trade unions from being sued by employers because there were a number of challenges to the 1906 Trade Disputes Act, and that in itself was a good thing. The beginnings of case law are now starting to come through: in 1990 a company called River Valley, which employed an all-female staff organised by SIPTU, let the entire staff go and brought in mainly young males at about half the rate. Obviously a dispute took place because people wanted their jobs back, and when SIPTU called for a boycott of the products of the company they were quickly injuncted and had to withdraw their offer of support. When the workers went out and circulated leaflets asking for support for their cause, they were also injuncted, although it was settled out of court. But the act can prevent workers disseminating information about their problem, and the act can be used against workers in legitimate trade disputes.

I am personally very interested by what is happening in Europe and what way European trade unions deal with their employers, because their legislation is light years ahead of ours. We're basically in our infancy, with guidelines instead of laws.

Our union represents quite a large number of employees in transnational companies here and, in particular, there are a couple of large French companies that own several financial institutions here that I organise. We have contacted the French trade unions and, with their assistance and the assistance of French legislation, we did succeed in acquiring quite a lot of information about the companies' plans in Ireland and where they intended to go. The international board of the company met my union and gave us quite a lot of assurances in relation to the future and what they intended to do.

We have developed that link and the union which organises in Ireland and the UK is now developing a confederation with the French trade unions and other relevant unions, because I think that's the only way in Ireland that we are going to get information – in one instance at a meeting we were more informed of the company's intentions in Ireland than the local management we were dealing with. That turned the relationship around, and so much so that that company now calls an international meeting once a year between all its trade union representatives within Europe and their managing directors and spends two days dealing with any questions or queries that arise.

It is a powerful way of dealing with a company insofar as you can get the information. Now what we do with that information is that it is discussed, it is brought back to local level, and then we negotiate how a particular change happens or how we do that. And there's nothing unhealthy about that. That is what should be happening, because if people understand that they have a future with an organisation then they tend, at the end of the day, to fit in with that. If an employer has a head on his shoulders, he will consult heavily with the unions and allow them to influence what happens. The more open management is, the better communications are, the better the relationships are.

But it's obvious that the crucial thing is the quality of the information. I believe that the only place you are really going to get that information is on the board and that we should have a say there. In any company the management and the investors are only one half of the ingredients of success. The workforce is the other. If the workforce is not co-operating, then there are serious problems within that organisation. And it's not that we want to take anything away from the company. We are participating in that company.

Of course, I've mainly been talking about transnational companies. When you get down to your indigenous Irish company, it's a completely different ball game. We are somewhere in the middle ages in relation to dealing with them, and the smaller the company the worse the relationships are. There is still the attitude: "Who the hell do you think you are? You have no right to interfere."

There is no conception or acceptance of the fact that the workforce is the other half of this business. What we've seen happen to Waterford Glass is a prime example of where business decisions were taken that turned out to be a disaster for the company. There's a lot of anger, even hatred, among the workforce for what happened in that company, but it is the workers who are paying an enormous price for what happened. And, at the end of the day, that's who does pay.

Looking to the future, I think the best way forward for the trade union movement lies in linking in with the European trade union movement in trying to develop that EC directive. I don't think we can wait for Irish employers to see the light. They won't; they don't want to. I think we can make progress with large transnational companies once they have a trade union base in Europe, and we can use either the German, French, or whatever legislation is there, in the meantime, until the directive becomes law.

At the end of the day, I am sad to say, I am not optimistic about anything homegrown and think we have to look to Europe if we are to get proper legislation to have some say in our destiny in working for an employer.

Susan O'Keeffe

I'LL START BY saying I don't eat beef anymore; haven't eaten beef since the programme went out. It has become part of my life in a way I never anticipated.

When I started out looking at the Goodman group of companies and the beef industry in Ireland, I was working as a business journalist and I specialised in the agri-business sector, and so I was well aware of the power of the Goodman group. I was aware of their PR machine. I was aware of their public image. I was aware of the attitude of government towards Goodman – indeed, it could be argued, that the government thought that Goodman equalled God at the time. It was a little, as Mary Raftery has said, like Paddy Gallagher. People thought he had the golden touch.

The meat business is a very complex business and so it was very easy to walk away from it if you wanted to. It is complicated further by EC regulation and by Irish legislation. There was very little to encourage someone like me, or anybody else, to pursue a company like this, or to research it, because it was just plain difficult. There were lots of obstacles in the way and, as Mary Raftery and others have said, it's normal for companies in Ireland to say nothing. Even if they have good news, they find it hard to talk. But if there's anything at all going on that they don't want you to know about, they are certainly not going to assist you and they are not legally obliged to.

I was also aware that the Goodman group of companies had successfully over the years pushed a lot of writs out and made it difficult for journalists to pursue any sort of story. There was lots of innuendo, there was lots of pub gossip. There was nothing concrete at all. Goodman also had plenty of enemies. You know, people who loved to talk to me and say, "Oh, wait till I tell you what Mr Goodman did," or "Wait till I tell you this, that, and the other." There were also plenty of friends around who'd love to say, "Wait till I tell you what Mr Goodman did," or what he didn't do.

And all of this was bound up with a complete lack of any official kind of information, any official assistance, because as you know there's no freedom of information of any sort. And nobody wants to help you if you want to find out anything – I can say that as someone who tried and found that the system really doesn't help.

The other problem is that this is such a small country. Ireland is something that we can't escape from, in which everyone knows everybody else. I think there is a golden circle, but, even beyond the golden circle, people just know each other. They went to school with them, or they worked with them for a while, or they studied together, and you constantly keep coming up against people who say, "Oh yeah, I remember him," and then they are afraid to talk.

There were other obstacles – why be the first to say something? People I would approach for information would say, "Ah, you'd be better off saying nothing." And "Why should I be the one?" – very convenient arguments that lots of people like to hide behind. Even when I had one person who had actually spoken to me – who is known now as Patrick McGuinness – at that point he was still speaking in a private capacity, and so I couldn't go around and say to other people, "Oh well, there is somebody."

I was depending all the time on somebody speaking out and nobody wanted to, and it became clear to me that this wasn't just another company. There are lots of companies operating in this country. There seemed to be more at stake, and I wasn't quite clear at the start what those things were, although it became clearer to me as time passed. When people said to me, "I'll only meet you late at night," "I'll only meet you in a car park," or "I'll only meet you in some obscure bar in the middle of nowhere," I didn't think they had been watching too much television.

I genuinely believed that they were afraid of something, there was some reason for them to ask to meet me in this way, to give me coded messages, to make phone calls that didn't quite finish. They'd say, "Well, you know what I'm talking about," and "I'll see you then," and it was all obscure and odd. People would say to me, "I'm afraid of speaking. I'm afraid of giving you this." People were afraid of being threatened, of losing their jobs, of being followed.

They were just plain scared and that made me feel not very good, I have to say, because when you're all the time dealing with a huge level of fear, it makes you a bit afraid as well. And it certainly made me a bit afraid, even though I didn't know what I was afraid of. But if people keep telling you to be careful and keep saying they feel threatened then, inevitably, it rubs off.

I think in Ireland people are used to a kind of silent situation. It's much more comfortable to say nothing than it is to stand up and speak out. And those people I spoke to were people who were informed, who knew what was going on, and were scared of breaking that silence. It's like an unwritten rule: "You shall not break it; you shall not get involved." And if someone like me approaches you, for God's sake, say nothing; it's much safer.

And I'd go back to the same people again and say, "I've got a little bit more information this time. Do you think you could help me a little bit further than you did the last time?"

But even when you found them, you couldn't be guaranteed you'd get the right answer. And I had to. I was forced to on two levels. One was to look at basic facts like what colour is a box of meat, or what does it weigh, or what does it look like? So if a guy who was sitting in his kitchen at midnight told me a story about illegal boxing of meat that had gone on for days and days and he gave me great detail about how it had been done, I'd have to go then and work out exactly whether what he had said could be possible. Could you unpack that amount of meat in that space of time? Would it be possible? Would it all rot? Was what he was saying legitimate?

And they were only the basic small facts, but absolutely essential to a journalist. On top of that you had all the other stuff about bogus invoices, and rotten meat and intervention meat being sold to Iraq, and how would that work? How do you rebox meat and where do you rebox it? Under the table payments – how could that be possible?

Now all these things are familiar to anybody at all who has read a few reports from the beef tribunal. At the time when I was going through this, a lot of it was unfamiliar even to people who might have known a little bit about the company or the business, and it made it all very complicated for me, because people thought you must be making this up, or she's imagining things, or she'd like to believe all this is true. It just made it a much longer story to pursue because of that.

I found some people did have a lot to say, and I'm glad there are still people in this country who believe in telling the truth, who believe when they get an opportunity that you say what you know. Some of them were surprised at my level of *naïveté* because I would ask questions which showed obviously that I thought certain things were impossible. They'd say, "But yeah, of course it's possible to go to a bank and get loads of cash out of them without proper identification," or whatever. And I was saying, "It can't be possible. I never heard of it before. It's not supposed to be that way." And that, again, made it complicated. How was *I* going to prove any of this?

There were people who wanted money for information, and I think that's probably always the case. First of all, they never got it, and, secondly, whatever they might have had to say, I don't believe in paying for information. I don't think it's a valid way of getting information.

Some people were afraid of losing their job, or not being able to pay the mortgage, or not being able to send the children to school, and I understand that. That's why it's important that there are people who tell journalists what is really going on. Peter Murtagh and Joe Joyce, in their book *The Boss,* dedicated it to the people who really tell journalists what's going on, and I would like to echo that sentiment. But the group of people who bothered me the most in the entire eight months of investigating the beef industry were the group who kept saying to me, "Ah, you know, you shouldn't be talking about this at all. It's much better, now, for the good of Ireland that you should say nothing at all." And that really bothered me, because I knew that they knew certain things had happened, and I knew they had happened, and I knew some of them were wrong. I also knew that some of those issues had been raised in the public arena, notably in Dáil Éireann, and had been denied, or fudged, and it was much easier for these people to blame me. They'd call me a traitor and that was much easier for them to say.

And then they'd say, "You don't really care about Ireland; you don't care about the beef industry; you don't care about the workers." It was all terribly easy for them to say. What they found harder to accept was that the good of Ireland can only be strengthened if business becomes more honest and if politicians tell the truth and if, when things have gone wrong, they are acknowledged, and if there is proper accountability.

These people didn't want to talk about such things at all; they just wanted to say to me, "Stop, go away, leave it alone, it's much better the way it is."

I do care about the way Ireland is. I do care about the good of Ireland. I wouldn't have bothered going to all that effort if I didn't care. It would be much easier to join the silent ranks and say nothing at all. We will have strength if things are honest. A business built on lies will fall apart eventually.

It was difficult to investigate in this country. It was difficult to pursue facts; it was difficult to get anyone to talk. All that time you had the feeling that the official policy everywhere was to say nothing. It was a selective thing. The Department of Agriculture doesn't like giving out information and it's not their position to give out information. The IDA is much the same. The Revenue Commissioners, the customs, the Gardaí, none of the ordinary state organisations are into it. It's not the way their culture operates.

And then, individual civil servants are bound by the Official Secrets Act even if you get through the official barrier. The bankers, accountants and solicitors, and so on, are obviously bound by client confidentiality. And it began to seem to me that everyone was bound by something. Nobody bound by the truth. Or very few people seemed to think that the truth was the thing that mattered the most.

And I remember at one point the IDA actually saying, although this was before I started into the preparation for this programme, that their official policy now was to say nothing at all about the Goodman company. I thought that that was very interesting. How on earth had they come up with such a policy? Who sits on the board of the IDA? Who funds the IDA? Who does it work for? It works for you and me, and it's paid for by taxpayers, and somebody somewhere had decided, right or not, that "We're not saying anything more. I don't care who rings up, tell them we're saying nothing."

I have to say I found that quite shocking. I think the IDA has over the years adopted a policy of building up a kind of a wall of silence when something goes wrong with a company. If they've got a good announcement, everybody goes to lunch – I've been there, and they have a very nice canteen.

But when things go wrong, instead of standing up and saying, "Listen, we can't be responsible for everything that goes on in those companies. We do our best to try and keep a track of it, and we don't want this to go on, and we'd like to see change," they go completely silent, and, in doing so, they are hand in hand with the business community. The relationship between the IDA and businesses is a snapshot of the way government and business act in this country – after all, the IDA is an extension of the state; it's not an independent body. And I don't believe they are acting in our interests – and I don't mean to pick on the IDA as the only one, there are plenty of other semi-state organisations who behave in the same way, but the IDA is probably the biggest.

At the end of the day, they probably do whatever they like. If they decide on a policy of silence, who's going to challenge them? Who's going to say you can't do that? Nobody does. And even when I wrote about that at the time, it didn't change anything. And then of course we had the episode of cabinet confidentiality – who are the cabinet? Who pays their salary and who are they making these decisions on behalf of? I thought it was on behalf of you and me. But clearly I was wrong.

There were days in the eight months when I did this programme when I genuinely thought I should give up. I should stop. I wasn't making any progress. It was a brick wall. The system was bigger than me. It was more powerful. They were too clever, too strong. They'd been at it a lot longer than me. All the odds were stacked on their side and not on mine. And also, there was another distressing question. If I was trying to succeed where I knew other people had failed to tell the story about Goodman and his group of companies – and they had failed for all kinds of reasons – who on earth was I to make a difference?

At the end of the day, I had to fall back on the sources I had and think, there is a small group of people out there who have told me things and I don't want to let them down. I'm only a messenger after all. I didn't see or take part in any of the things I reported on, like any journalist. And if people wanted to trust me and believed that I wouldn't let them down, then I couldn't let them down, so I couldn't walk away from it. If I'd given people my word that I would never fail them as a source, then I was never going to do that. It's difficult but you do it.

If the price of not revealing a source is going to prison: well, it isn't difficult for me. I'll go to prison if that's what the system offers me because I'm not going to give away my sources. I hope nothing ever happens to make me. I couldn't walk away from what they said and I couldn't breach their confidence and, if going to prison for a day or a week or a month is the price of getting things out in the open, I think it's a price worth paying. I believe there are other journalists in this country and in the world who believe also that that price is worth paying. I've never tasted prison, but I'm prepared to try it if I have to.

I would like to take issue with people who have questioned my loyalty to Ireland. I think it was a shame that some people fell into the trap of thinking that because this programme was produced by a British television company that it had less value, and that somehow I was a traitor. The Goodman group of companies was operating in a European context anyway! I think it is sad that it wasn't done here. I did try to bring the story out here. It didn't work out. I think, I hope, we're better off for having had the story come out somewhere, and I have to say about *World in Action* that it is an office where people never say, "Oh, I wonder whose toes that'll tread on," or "That's a bit dangerous." I never ever heard that. If a story is sound, if you have the ingredients, if you can get to the bottom of it, then you're allowed to tell that story, and I'm glad that resource is there. I wish there was an equivalent resource like that in Ireland.

And, at the end, people have asked me lots of times what I thought the programme had achieved. Was it worth it? Would I do it all again? Yes, I would do it all again. Even though it was bloody difficult, and even though people put obstacles in my way – and there's no doubting that – I think it was worth it because I think it has forced certain matters out into the open. Not enough, in my opinion, but you have to start somewhere. It has forced us ordinary people to question matters which we thought were OK. I think maybe we're not as willing or as ready to accept the status quo now as we were. But at the end I think the thing that it achieved is that the veil of secrecy or of silence can be lifted. It's bloody difficult, but it can be done and it should be done. I hope that after that story and all the other ones that we've seen that, as Michael Mills has said, the trend will continue and not be reversed.

Michael Mills

PERHAPS I SHOULD refer briefly to the fact that since the tribunal was set up, so many people have been complaining about the cost of the tribunal, and that, unfortunately, includes some journalists. It's a very glib response to a situation which arose originally through the programme created by Susan O'Keeffe and which has over the past year or more led to an amount of very disturbing evidence being produced. I think anybody who talks in terms of cost for a tribunal of this sort, as against the absolute need to establish the truth, is talking very glibly and without due regard for the welfare of the country.

We've listened for two hours to a series of most thought-provoking contributions. I think it's fair to say that you probably will not see in our time again a collection of people of the dedication and the commitment of the journalists, the academics, the odd politician such as Garret FitzGerald, and a trade unionist like John Tierney, of people like Carl Bernstein and Salman Rushdie. Because there is a belief sometimes, as Susan O'Keeffe has mentioned, that you can't fight the system. You can fight the system. Don't ever let anybody be disposed to believe that you can't fight the system. It doesn't matter how strong it is. Woodward and Bernstein proved that in the case of the establishment in the United States, the strongest establishment in the world. And the truth has to be searched out and exposed. This meeting should not just be thought-provoking. We shouldn't go away and forget about or fail to take action in respect of many of the ideas that have been put forward. When I was talking some months ago about the need for a freedom of information act, one senior journalist who is a very good person said to me, "But what do I do about it? I write one article and then it's forgotten about."

Now, I hate to tell journalists how to do their work, but there is a system of lobbying involved. That's what it's all about. It's about a consistent and systematic campaign carried out over a long period of time, and I think the first thing you do is that you take the best of what you can from the contributions that have been made here and you study the legislation in other parts of the world that relate to freedom of information. What we're looking for and what you're looking for is not something unique. It's available.

Freedom of information legislation is available in most civilised countries in the world and you might, with benefit, look at the legislation in the United States. You might also look at the legislation in Australia and in New Zealand. Access to information and the rights of persons seeking information are the responsibility of the Ombudsman in New Zealand, and that's a very effective method of ensuring that the public service by the political officers respond to the need for information to be made available.

PUBLISH AND BE BANNED

Steve MacDonogh

A LARGE PANOPLY OF laws bears upon the book publisher, and in the last ten or more years I have had to take a crash course in the law. As a publisher I am publishing for Ireland, but I am also publishing internationally, and particularly for Britain. So it is that the experience that I am going to relate involves both British and Irish law. Censorship knows no boundaries, and all states have their provisions and the mentalities behind those provisions express themselves in remarkably similar language.

One of the first books we took on at Brandon was called *British Intelligence and Covert Action*. Aware that it posed certain legal problems, we took legal advice in London both in relation to libel and the Official Secrets Act, and we were satisfied that after slight amendment and careful phrasing the book would be safe from prosecution. The particular difficulty was that 120 members, or probable members, of the British Intelligence Services were listed in an appendix to the book with brief biographies. And the publication, in bringing together such a listing, was, to my knowledge, unprecedented.

The D-Notice Committee in London wrote to us asking to see a copy. This committee is a committee of the Department of Defence, which has actually no legal powers to ban books, but which writes to publishers of books and magazines and to newspapers and programme makers, advising them that it would not be a good idea to proceed with publication. And pretty well every book that has been published on British Intelligence in the last 50 years has gone through this voluntary censorship process. We, however, took the line that it was not our concern to provide them with an opportunity to censor our book.

We received from the D-Notice Committee a letter which complained that our book constituted "an extensive and serious breech of D-Notice Number 6 in publishing detailed information about the activities and methods of the Security and Intelligence services." There then followed a period when Margaret Thatcher, who was Prime Minister at that time, commissioned a report about the possibility of drafting new legislation in light of the fact that this book had slipped through the net, and this report was to be drafted jointly by the Prime Minister's office, the Foreign Office and the Ministry of Defence.

News of the possible drafting of new legislation was carried in British newspapers in March 1984, just as we were about to publish a new edition of the book. In early April the London *Times* published an editorial headed "Secrets Which Should Be Kept". It named our book, said its publication was indefensible, and supported the suppression of such material.

We found ourselves in an awkward situation, as the presses were rolling with copies of the re-issue. We were a small, new company which couldn't possibly afford to have thousands of books sitting in a warehouse unable to be sold. I was advised by lawyers and political advisers that a new law could be introduced in approximately 48 hours in the House of Commons, given that they would be invoking national security. So I let it be known to several journalists who were believed to be linked to the Intelligence establishment that we had abandoned plans for a reprint. Meanwhile, we delivered books into British bookshops. When we held a press conference in the House of Commons in May, it was too late for them to stop us.

While the preparation of new legislation continued, however, another form of action was taken. One of the authors of *British Intelligence and Covert Action* was Jonathan Bloch, a South African refugee. We had published the book in May 1983. In December 1983, he was denied permanent residency in Britain. He had been a political activist in South Africa, and if he was sent back there it was quite clear that he would be in serious difficulties. In May 1984 there was an early day motion in support of him in the House of Commons. But in June, his appeal against their refusal to allow him permanent residency was rejected.

It was an appalling situation. He was advised that he should appeal, but the finding of the adjudicator to whom he appealed was that the legislation did not allow the appeal to be decided in his favour. The Home Office had stated quite clearly their grounds for refusing him permission to remain in Britain. They said, "As you know, Mr Bloch is the co-author of a book entitled *British Intelligence and Covert Action* which contained the names of individuals allegedly working for British Intelligence authorities. Such an action is, in the view of the Secretary of State, bound to place servants of the Crown at greater risk of harm, whether or not the allegations are well-founded than had the book not been published." They had failed to stop the book but they were determined to exact revenge on one of the authors.

The persecution of Jonathan Bloch continued. In November '84, the second appeal was refused, and when they refused the second appeal they added further stings:

You will recall that your client had an application in in 1982 for an indefinite leave to remain and was refused because of his co-authorship of a book called *British Intelligence and Covert Action*. The Secretary of State understands that since your client was refused indefinite leave to remain on 22nd December, 1983, the book has been republished in England and a Russian edition of 100,000 copies was to be published by the Soviet Politisdat publishing house.

The Secretary of State continues to take the view that your client's co-authorship of the book is bound to place at greater risk of harm servants of the Crown, whether or not the allegations in the book are well founded. In the view of the Secretary of State this risk is increased by the greater circulation the book will now enjoy. Further, the Secretary of State has taken into account information about your client's association with persons whose activities, in the opinion of the Secretary of State, are prejudicial to the interests of the United Kingdom.

Totally unsubstantiated allegations were being made about Jonathan Bloch's associations and he was denied access to a hearing in any court of law or even administrative tribunal at which the truth or otherwise of the allegations could be tested. The names of the "dubious" people with whom he was supposed to be associating were never given. The state was not required to argue its case in any way.

Prior to publication our legal advice had been that no breaches of the law would be committed and the state never indicated that it disagreed with this legal opinion. Jonathan Bloch was never interviewed by the police or any other state authority about the publication of the book or even about his alleged associations. His process of appeals went on with further rejections in 1985 and 1986. Finally, a compromise was arrived at and he continues to live in Britain but no longer writes about British Intelligence.

The second book where we ran into some trouble was a book called *British Military Strategy in Northern Ireland*, published in 1984. This time it was a question of libel, and we learnt a salutary lesson as regards the laws of libel.

A genuine error was made in this book. The author had made a simple slip in taking notes and had confused two organisations. One was a genuine sociological research organisation, the other was a name of convenience used by British Military Intelligence. The book therefore contained a grave and serious error and had to be withdrawn two weeks after publication and pulped. In this instance we could have no complaint.

The following year we published a book called *My Story* by Joanne Hayes. Two teams of lawyers studied and read it and reported on it and suggested changes. Senior counsel remarked on how very restrained Joanne Hayes was in her remarks on her treatment at the hands of the law. I can't go into great detail about this case, but in the end of the day £100,000 in damages and costs were paid out. In the year in which we published that book our total turnover was only £100,000. The consequence was two years of living on the brink of extinction, of waking up every morning and not knowing whether or not you will be able to continue.

In trying to keep the company alive in circumstances which should have ruined us, I was made painfully aware of how isolated we were. There was a total lack of support available. It is a hard enough business to pursue successfully as it is, to try to build up a company from scratch. Most publishers live off books they published years ago, but a newcomer cannot do so.

The energies used up in fighting various cases were energies which should have been devoted to the publication of books and the marketing and promotion of them. There was no civil liberties body, or freedom of expression body, or group or union, no form of support for anyone finding themselves in such a situation.

The following year – 1986 – we published a book called *One Girl's War*. After publishing *British Intelligence and Covert Action*, I had not been particularly interested in publishing another book on British Intelligence despite receiving an enormous number of manuscripts on the subject. I turned them all down until this one came in. It didn't tell anything new about British Intelligence, but we decided to publish it because it was a genuine story in terms of British wartime nostalgia of a slightly feckless young woman running around London having a jolly good war, thank you very much; having nice cups of tea while listening to the bombs falling, and, meanwhile, succeeding in being a key witness in a major spy trial.

We published *One Girl's War* despite the knowledge that it had been dropped from the list of Weidenfeld and Nicholson following a rather strange correspondence. The book had been submitted to the D-Notice Committee, which had passed it. The author had also received verbal assurances from her former employers in MI5 that it was OK to publish it. However, the Treasury Solicitor, representing the government, wrote to Weidenfeld and Nicholson suggesting that the book might result in a prosecution under the Official Secrets Act.

This was in 1984, before the Peter Wright business. Our legal advice was that the threats from the Treasury Solicitor were bogus, that it would be entirely unprecedented if an action were brought, and highly unlikely that any action could succeed under the Official Secrets Act. We were advised that it was safe to go ahead. However, when we published in 1986 we were hit with injunctions in Dublin and London.

On the Thursday we knew about the Irish injunction, and on the Monday we were in the High Court in Dublin. The resources of the British state are not inconsiderable. Those of a small publishing company are rather different, but we decided to fight it and we were lucky enough to get an excellent judgement.

The state of the law in practice has a lot to do with the extent to which cases are fought. If you don't fight cases, you don't create precedent. We don't know the limits, we haven't tested the limits of freedom of expression under the Constitution. However, in this case – it was a rare case in which precedent was set – the British legal journal *Public Law* reported the Brandon success as "an important blow for freedom of the press in Ireland. In view of the emphatic manner in which Carroll J. upheld the right to communicate, it would probably be only in exceptional circumstances that the Irish courts would restrain the publication of material which a government found embarrassing or disclosure of which was deemed to be contrary to the public interest."

Despite our succcess in Dublin, we were now faced with an injunction in London, restraining our distributors. To cut a long story short, we made strenuous efforts to try to raise the funds to be able to allow our distributors to contest a full hearing in London. I contacted the NUJ and the leadership took copies of the book and said they would get back to me. I'm still waiting. I wrote to every major book publishing company in Britain through the Publishers' Association in Britain. I got one reply which said that they had enough problems of their own, thank you very much. I went to London to meet a civil liberties lawyer and to discuss the situation with the editors of some of the newspapers. No support was forthcoming.

Part of the reason why they would not lend support had to do with the fact that the book was not a book of great substance. And I think that's important when looking at the question of how one fights or does not fight in terms of freedom of expression. It's important to recognise that the battle that has to be fought may not be on the territory that you would have chosen if you had the choice.

As far as I am concerned, it was quite clear that Margaret Thatcher's government was pursuing a wide principle in relation to the suppression of information regarding the Intelligence service. She was pursuing that principle in looking for the drafting of new legislation when we published *British Intelligence and Covert Action*. She was pursuing that principle when the Treasury Solicitor sought the suppression of our book *One Girl's War*, and she later pursued the same principle in relation to Peter Wright. The question of the substance of the contents of the book was neither here nor there in my opinion, but left and liberal opinion in Britain tended to say that they would rather wait until there was left-wing or other progressive opinion being suppressed.

Our book was that of a loyal servant of the Crown, Joan Miller; it was a conservative book, with no left-wing agenda. But I can think of no surer recipe for self-defeat than to say you will only defend the freedom of expression of those with whom you agree.

It proved impossible to get any support from anyone to fight the case in Britain, and so for six years it stood. However, in 1992 I wrote to the Treasury Solicitor saying that it was my intention to present myself in London with copies of the book and sell them in defiance of the law, and if they wished to act upon the injunction which was still in force we would pursue them through the European courts. They said that they would insist upon the injunction but in fact, the day before I flew to London, they crumbled and agreed in principle to discharge the injunction.

That injunction has now been discharged and they have admitted that they were wrong in law all the time. However, they are now threatening to prosecute us under the 1989 legislation which has been introduced since our publication. So, in a couple of weeks I will be going to London again, clutching copies of *One Girl's War* and offering them for sale and offering the British government the opportunity to intervene with the law again.*

In 1986 we published *The Politics of Irish Freedom* by Gerry Adams and sought to advertise it on RTE radio. The ad simply mentioned the author and title of the book. It was rejected.

In 1992 we published a book of short stories called *The Street and Other Stories* by Gerry Adams. We again submitted an ad to RTE, who refused to broadcast it. First of all they said they wouldn't broadcast it because Gerry Adams's voice was to be used. They changed their minds and said that they would refuse to broadcast any ad for the book, whatever it said and whoever it was spoken by.

It is important to understand the kind of thinking that underlies the decisions of our broadcasting organisations. This is from an affidavit in the case:

It is the view of RTE that to broadcast any statement whatsoever, on any subject, by Mr Adams would amount, in effect, to the broadcasting of propaganda on behalf of Sinn Féin. Where his utterances touch on political matters they are clearly related to the affairs of Sinn Féin. If they touch on other matters, it is clear that they will have the effect of better publicising Gerry Adams and his reputation generally and thereby making the message which he carries on behalf of Sinn Féin more acceptable to the public at large.

*The Attorney General, again one day before he was due to arrive in London, conceded Steve MacDonogh's point, agreed not to invoke official secrets legislation against him, and paid damages to Turnaround Distribution, Brandon's British distributors.

In the current context, the publication of a book of short stories can only have, or be reasonably construed as having, the aim of portraying Mr Adams as an artist, a man of culture, and a man who writes stories which by their nature are intended to enable the readers to identify with both the story, and by inference the writer and the message it conveys.

It is RTE's view that any attempt by Mr Adams, or any attempt by persons on his behalf to promote his own image in this way, can only have as its aim the advancement of the cause of Sinn Féin, and by reason of the facts that have been established in evidence before the High Court and the Supreme Court of this state that that organisation is committed to the dismantling of the organs of state by violent and unconstitutional methods, that the broadcasting of any material of this nature emanating from Mr Adams, or any material whatsoever, must be reasonably regarded as highly likely to promote or incite to crime or tend to undermine the authority of the state.

That comes from our "national" broadcasting organisation. It doesn't come from the government, it doesn't come from the state seeking to use the law to defend itself against politically evil opponents who are prepared to use violence. It comes from a broadcasting organisation, and I must say that I thought the business of a broadcasting organisation was to broadcast and to defend the context in which their employees go about their business, to make it more possible for them to do their job better all the time.

It should be the business of broadcasting authorities to defend freedom of expression rather than to seek to limit it. But RTE is like a prisoner with gate fever. When the recent High Court decision showed them a chink of light of the door opening slightly they slammed the door shut quickly and said, "No, no, keep me inside please."

Brandon Book Publishers is seeking a judicial review in the High Court of the decisions of RTE and the IRTC, which followed suit, with a view to establishing our right to free expression in promoting our books.* I started Brandon in 1982. Ten years later

---

*In the High Court in July 1993 Mr Justice Paul Carney ruled that RTE were better able to judge whether the advertisement should be broadcast than the courts.

what you could call "one publisher's war" continues. I don't think that it should be so difficult to publish. I don't think that one should have to be engaged in legal battles to defend the right to publish the kind of material we have published. In terms of British secrets, I would certainly contend that it is extremely important that the British people know what is being perpetrated in their name by their Intelligence service.

The timing of this conference is fortunate. Whatever one thinks of programmes for government, there is a sense in which we live in days of hope. The big attendance at this conference is an indication that there will be sufficient pressure brought to bear on the government that we will be able to free up, in some regard, anyway, the current panoply of obstacles to a freely informed public. Because, in the end of the day, it's not the publishers who matter so much, not even the writers who matter so much. At the end of the day it's the readers who matter, the readers' access to information.

Maxine Brady

I HAVE TO say that it is unusual to be speaking at this particular venue without a block of Youth Defence and friends of Youth Defence sitting over there to disrupt my speech and the proceedings.

It's almost a year since the infamous X case, a year which at times has been very painful for people, often fantastic, and in many respects has been highly entertaining. I don't want to restate the obvious in my address but to make it very clear why USI* took the controversial stance that it did, and to share with you some of the funnier moments that we've encountered along the way.

USI and other student unions quietly distributed information on abortion pre and post the 1983 referendum with little interference and with even less attention. Even then there were plans eventually to stop us as we were seen to be a serious threat because of our undermining of the Eighth Amendment to the Constitution.

What exactly is abortion information? SPUC** and other anti-abortion groups will define it as information on murder. A premise, I believe, that is perfectly acceptable to someone whose morals, conscience and religious leaders dictate that opinion to them. Yet across the world most countries have legalised abortion simply because it is not viewed as murder, and in no other country has information on abortion been restricted or banned as this country has managed to do.

At USI we publish in our national newspaper and welfare guide the addresses and telephone numbers of consultation clinics in Britain, where in having consultation you may arrange, if you so wish, a termination of your pregnancy. We do not, have not and will not refer women directly to abortion clinics, despite allegations to the contrary.

The two countries that we refer women to for consultations are Britain and Holland (the reason we refer to the Netherlands is because many women who have come to us have been subject to pro

*The Union of Students in Ireland.
**Society for the Protection of Unborn Children.

hibition orders and are not allowed to enter the UK). The laws of both countries dictate that all potential patients for termination of pregnancy must go through at least a consultative process or a counselling process. And it is ironic that had the forces of SPUC and the state not combined to close down many of our centres for pregnancy counselling, many of the trips to England by so many Irish women would not have been made. For many counsellors and counselling agencies here, the risk of legal action and the financial penalties that entailed were just too big for the agencies involved. And so USI and other member student unions were the most likely successors to the clinics, who were forced to close down their pregnancy counselling facilities. While we were by no means the only source of information, we were by far the most vocal, the most confrontational. In 1988 and 1989 we were all very young. Many of the student defenders had just left their teens behind them. We were full of youthful idealism and principles and, most importantly, in our opinion SPUC was demeaning us as individuals.

Like Steve MacDonogh, we were far from rich – as a matter of fact, we were penniless and most of us were in debt already. We had no assets, no property, no money, only one of us had a dependent, and we were far from embarking upon our careers, and indeed many of us still are far from embarking upon our careers.

However, what made the students' idealism take them into battle was our determination that SPUC would not intimidate us or halt what we viewed as a basic human right and an essential aspect of our welfare services for women students. I firmly believe that one of the major mistakes made by the "masterminds of the right", to quote Emily O'Reilly, was their belief that they could frighten the students into submission. What they didn't bank on was a student population protective of their leadership, their interests, and, above all, their autonomy and democratic structures.

Their second major mistake was to think that they could achieve a blanket prohibition on abortion information. We live in the 1990s, an era of fax machines, photocopiers, computer link-ups, television, satellites and a refusal by many individuals across the world and many organisations across the world to submit to censorship. It would be impossible to achieve a blanket prohibition of abortion information.

It was never our intention to become pregnancy counsellors, nor was it our function to break the law just for the hell of it, but we did take on the role of counsellors and we did take on the role of law-breakers. Year after year, in college after college, students voted and mandated USI to continue to break the law, breach injunctions and give support and assistance to Irish women with crisis pregnancies. To those who have accused us of being undemocratic, I say majority votes are the basis of democracies worldwide. The majority of students in this country voted to support USI out of a compassion for the dilemma many of the women frequently find themselves in.

In reality SPUC were their own worst enemy. The publicity generated around court actions they initiated against the students ensured that women knew where to get the information they often so desperately wanted. On average we would receive three to four calls a week, but every time we went to court or distributed *USI News* the number of calls would triple.

When the European Court of Justice delivered its opinion against us in October of 1991, within an hour of the news breaking our phone lines were constantly busy with abortion information. On that particular day we counselled and informed 15 women, all at various stages of pregnancy, of all ages and under many different circumstances. Quite often over the past four years women have cried on the phone when someone has simply said, "Yes, we give information on abortion."

As the controversy grew and more and more learnt that we would help we became more than pregnancy counsellors. In many respects we became a rape crisis centre, a marriage guidance centre, someone to talk to about family problems for young people, the Samaritans, and, above all, a family planning clinic. The shocking thing about all of it was the reality of crisis pregnancies within this state.

Many of our callers were middle-aged and often middle-class married women, some of whose contraception had failed, and all too many schoolgirls under the age of sixteen. But the majority were not, as SPUC would insist on having you believe, young women who were selfish in their career prospects and who did not want to leave college. Each of those women had a different reason. Each of them, in my opinion, viewed her dilemma as life-threatening, in the broader sense of the word.

There was a number of cases which were particularly poignant and difficult to deal with for those of us who weren't professional counsellors but nevertheless had to take on the burden of trying to be professional and responsible to women in crisis.

There was one woman whose abusive husband had left her. Her in-laws blamed her for the break-down of the marriage and she had been estranged from her own family for many years. Her first pregnancy had been difficult and the delivery had almost killed her. Her obstetrician had advised her not to become pregnant again as she might not survive the delivery. She did of course become pregnant again after a brief reunion with her husband. She discovered the pregnancy at four weeks. Both her obstetrician and her GP advised termination, but they couldn't and they wouldn't tell her how to go about achieving a termination of pregnancy. It took her six weeks to discover that USI would help.

Her reasons for her termination were very simple. She did not want to take the risk of seriously damaging her health or dying, and she did not want to leave her four-year-old child alone. That woman felt she had no other option and could anyone in justice deny her that option and her right to take it? Did we ever, and do we ever have the right to deny her information, and other women like her?

Not all of our callers were in such difficult circumstances. We had one particular young woman who was frightened at the prospects of telling her parents and concerned about the effect the child would have upon her career and college. She came for counselling, was referred to the professionals and was given information not only on abortion, which we did for every woman who came to us, but adoption, foster care, childcare and benefit entitlements.

She returned last September to USI with her six-week-old baby and was adamant that had she not been given the opportunity to talk she would have terminated that pregnancy. Her life isn't by any means easy, but she is enjoying her son and she's happy, although she's very often broke because the state does not support single mothers adequately.

Many of the women who called couldn't speak the word abortion, such was the guilt that this society has foisted upon them. They asked for family planning information or they would hang up. We all became adept at deciphering and interpreting their words and the weird and wonderful substitutes for the word abortion. As we became known as a point of contact, women would sometimes call to the door with their husbands and ask to see someone.

It's ironic and not very well known, but in the basement of 16 North Great George's Street USI are based beside NAOMI, the National Association for the Ovulation Method in Ireland. Many NAOMI clients when they called to the door would recoil in horror when innocently asked, "Is it abortion information you're looking for?"

I believe that in USI we played an essential role throughout the period. We know that we helped many women not only getting their abortion but to keep their babies, and we know that our radicalism and our idealism was in many ways a major factor in creating change both in terms of law and in terms of public opinion.

I won't raise the general legal arguments, but there are, however, several points to be made which concern me greatly. When the "X" case rocked not only this country but the rest of the world, the secrets of the Irish negotiating team to the Maastricht Treaty began to come out. Protocol 17, with its possible effects on Irish women, became an issue of public debate, as it should have been right from the start. The government tried to appease the disquiet with a solemn declaration, assuring everyone that it had legal standing and would come into immediate effect on 18 June should the people ratify the treaty. If you remember, the declaration guaranteed that there would be no prosecutions or court actions against any women who travelled to England for abortions. It also guaranteed the right of women to receive information, and both Albert Reynolds and the Attorney General publicly declared that the solemn declaration had legal standing and that "X" wouldn't happen again and certainly wouldn't happen before the referendum within that year.

Yet when USI went again to the High Court in July of 1992, the solemn declaration was rejected as an argument. Someone got it wrong. Someone got it very wrong. Either the presiding judge, Fred Morris, did not take full cognisance of our arguments, or chief members of the last government misled the public in June of 1992. It's for others to determine which is the case. I have my own opinions.

More importantly, many have been under the impression that the referendum in November of 1992 legalised abortion information. Be under no illusions. The injunction granted against USI in August 1992 is permanent and covers everyone who has knowledge of it. That includes everyone in this room, everyone who has ever read a newspaper article or listened to any broadcast programmes on which it was discussed. The law cannot be changed or judged retrospectively.

USI's stance will be adjudicated upon in the Supreme Court when our appeal is heard on the basis of the law as it stood in 1989. I would submit that we have two contradictory amendments in our constitution. Which one takes precedence? And on which interpretation do we base laws and judgements? The blame for such a legal minefield is placed fairly and squarely with successive governments post-1983 who failed to legislate on foot of the Eighth Amendment. Hence legislation on foot of the 1992 Amendment is now critical. Failure to legislate adequately will result in more court actions and more injunctions, especially when the anti-abortion forces in this country begin to regroup.

Legislation, though, will not be enough. The permanent injunction against USI must be lifted, as well as the perpetual injunctions against Dublin Well Woman Centre and Open Line Counselling. The Eighth Amendment must be repealed if we are to be clear on the protection of pregnant women in our society, and we must examine our own hypocrisies and our own fear of being labelled. It's all very well to allow women to travel to England for abortions, and it's all very well to deal with our own hard cases. But what about the women from the poorer socio-economic backgrounds? Women who cannot afford the trip to England. We cannot just clarify the legalities, we must also face up to the social aspects of abortion and the surrounding issues.

We must determine why women terminate their pregnancies so often. And why so many women get pregnant despite their intentions, and, perhaps more importantly, we should also develop and mature as a nation to establish support networks for women who choose to keep their babies in spite of the odds. Across the world, abortion and the surrounding issues have caused controversy and polarised societies. There are extremists on both sides. And such extremism in my opinion can be very dangerous. The call from some for unlimited abortion on demand with no time limit is both inhuman and abhorrent.

Abortion is not an easy nor is it a pleasant option. But it is very often a necessary one. On the other hand you cannot imprison women in the state for the duration of their childbearing years. Very often demands by extremists of the anti-abortion lobby border upon Disneyland creations. Women have always found ways to terminate unwanted pregnancies. A total ban on abortion information and travel will also have to ban the collection of a particular strain of seaweed we find around these shores. On 1 January of this year, all the redundant customs officers would have had to have been redeployed into the foetal police, and while these may be unlikely and fantastic scenarios, who would have thought that a year ago we would have hauled before the courts a fourteen-year-old schoolgirl? Extremism disguised as principle cannot be imposed upon the rest of society through laws and policies.

For me as an individual, and not just as the president of USI, the battle is far from over. There is still the question of costs. In 1989 the student leaders divested themselves of assets and ensured that we were written out of any wills or testaments. Until our costs are settled we will be unable to secure mortgages. We may still face bankruptcy proceedings. Those of us who are still union officers are still in contempt of court, and SPUC has threatened to appoint receivers to the three student unions involved to seize the costs.* Such a move will financially destroy the students union, be it be at UCD, Trinity or USI.

Whether or not the costs have eventually to be paid by the individuals or the unions, the students should not be left to pay them alone. We took on the job and role of pregnancy counselling centres when others could not and sometimes would not. Ideally, these costs should be borne by the state. But the reality is we will be asking people like you to dig deep into your pockets and help pay the costs.

To conclude, I would like to personalise what USI's experience has been through the abortion information battle. The experience has taught me a lot about humanity, about being young and Irish in the 20th century. And, above all else, about the law. Like Steve MacDonogh, I've taken a crash course in the law and have become *au fait* with injunctions and court proceedings. Over the past four

*At the time of going to press USI and Trinity students union are expecting seizure of their assets by sheriff's officers.

years, my ability to mother my daughter has been called into question – a strange contradiction, as I wouldn't have been allowed an abortion either. My sexuality, sexual integrity and reputation have been questioned, as has my mental stability. My actions have been called anarchic and reprehensible, which frankly I don't consider to be an insult. I was investigated along with the other 13 for corruption of public morals while attending ante-natal clinics. I've been called many things but through it all, Irish women and men and students supported me and my colleagues in USI, Trinity and UCD. The compassion and understanding that so many people felt for women was enlightening. I learnt pidgen English for the benefit of the foreign journalists who descended upon this country three times this year. It helped to try and unravel the tangles that we had woven in our own minds because many of the foreign journalists couldn't understand what the hell we were doing.

I have learnt how to listen and not to judge, which has stood me, and still does, in good stead. I've learnt to acknowledge that there are many people out there who are badly served by our society, numbed by inhibitions and guilt that are not theirs. Like the young woman who was having her fourth pregnancy terminated, who couldn't use contraceptives because it was against her religion. But most of all I've learnt to have a laugh at our very strange political quirks and to beat them at their own game. Threatened legal action may have removed books from our shelves in the libraries and censored magazines, but we knew that Easons still sold illegal books and we knew that Veritas sold the offending items as well, so we helped SPUC out to get them banned out of Veritas.

The seizing and the destruction of the *Guardian* was perhaps one of the funnier and lighter moments in the past year. The idea of police and customs officials waiting for an aeroplane to deliver a cargo of newspapers is too incredible to be anything other than hysterical.

Being Irish is something to be proud of. We're going through radical and dramatic social change. Women are coming to the forefront of political life, taking control of issues that affect them, and students are standing up to be counted and will not lie down. There can be little doubt that we have protected not only Irish women's rights, but the rights of millions of women in many countries. I believe that the stance taken by the USI is the right one and that stance has been vindicated. I believe that we were critical to the defeat of those seeking to control and manipulate legislative reform within this state.

I believe that the Union of Students of Ireland – and I'm saying this because I'm on my way out of USI and I think credit has to be paid to the students of this country – is to be applauded in its refusal to be dictated to or to accept laws that are wrong, unworkable, impractical and can never be enforced. USI will continue to break injunctions as long as the students mandate us to. We will continue to support Irish women in every way that we can; in light of the national referendum our campaign of civil disobedience may take a different tack but, as is expected of us, disobedient we will be.

While you deliberate today I urge you to remember and reflect that, according to the British Office of Statistics, at least 80 Irish women will travel to British abortion clinics next week – many of them still without information, alone, frightened and carrying the guilt of the nation, of this nation. For those women, and for the many others whose lives have been so drastically affected by censorship, we must not just talk, but this time we must act.

Damien Kiberd

THE LAST YEAR has seen a number of unusual, and, some would say, remarkable developments in the world of Irish journalism. Journalists have been threatened with jailing on several occasions for refusing to reveal their sources. They have been threatened with jail for the offence of criminal contempt. They have been threatened with jail for breaches of the Postal and Telecommunications Act 1983, and they have been legally restrained from publishing information which in other jurisdictions might come into the public domain as a matter of course.

The last year has also seen the concerted use of the legal system by both the political and the business establishment to prevent the disclosure of information and to muzzle criticism. As the number of legal battles increases between the pursuers and the pursued, it becomes apparent that the law, as it is constituted, offers a most dangerous framework which may be used most effectively by those who wish to conceal and to obscure, to run and to hide, and by those who wish to remain immune from the consequences of their actions.

I would like to deal with a number of practical issues which confront newspapers and broadcasters in their everyday work. The first I would like to go to is contempt of court, in our jurisdiction quite a serious crime. Depending on the attitude adopted by the authorities, a case may be referred either to the district court or to the circuit court. If a journalist is found guilty of the offence of contempt of court he or she may be liable in the district court to fines of up to £800 or six months in prison, or in the circuit court to fines of up to £10,000 or two years in jail.

There is no legal or constitutional protection for journalists who refuse to reveal their sources. The classic case in this area is that of Kevin O'Kelly of RTE, who refused to identify an interviewee so that he might be prosecuted by the authorities. It should be remembered that on that occasion the authorities secured a conviction of the defendant without the co-operation of the journalist, who refused to reveal his sources and instead went to jail.

Lately it has become clear to journalists that the legal obligation to disclose sources extends not just to the courts but to other bodies as well. Tribunals of inquiry and even the medical council may demand of journalists that they should reveal details of precisely who gave them information in regard to a story they published. This has led to the laughable situation on a number of occasions, where journalists who are hauled before such courts, tribunals, or councils are sometimes being interrogated by the very people who gave them the information in the first place.

Interrogators know that they can rely on the journalistic principle that the identity of the source will not be revealed and can freely berate the journalists, safe in the knowledge that the identity of the informant will not be disclosed.

When a priest is given confidential information in the confessional, or a garda is given confidential information by an informer, they may judiciously refrain from disclosing their sources. A journalist can enjoy no such protection. Ten months ago a reporter from the *Sunday Business Post* called Brian Carey and I were asked to reveal our sources by Justice Hamilton, the sole member of the beef tribunal. We refused. Justice Hamilton referred the case to the Director of Public Prosecutions. The reporter and I were questioned by gardaí from the Crime Branch of the Garda Síochána at their headquarters in the Phoenix Park. No charges have been laid against us in any court so far. We accepted this process as being quite normal and in accordance with the law. We had been in contempt of the tribunal. We referred our case to the High Court for judicial review and there Mr Justice Blaney held that the chairman of the Beef Tribunal was entitled to demand access to our sources, and I stress that we accepted all this as quite normal.

The most extraordinary development to emerge from this process, however, came some months later, when we received a letter from the chairman of the Beef Tribunal directing us to refer any information which might come our way and which might be relevant to the work of the tribunal through the tribunal in advance of publication. In a sense, the tribunal was saying that a newspaper with numerous curious reporters should, if it discovered something of or about the beef sector, convey that information to the tribunal in advance of publication.

The beef industry is an enormously important sector of the Irish economy and a business newspaper cannot avoid covering this sector, yet it is abundantly clear to us that every time a reporter runs a story on one of Ireland's biggest sectors, he or she also runs the risk of being hauled before the tribunal for interrogation. If the reporter refuses to disclose his or her sources, he or she may be liable to fining, to prosecution or to imprisonment.

The remit of the tribunal is wide. The chairman might decide that any issue relating to beef is within his mandate. Therefore, any reporter covering this sector should in theory never give an assurance of confidentiality to his source because that assurance can never be backed by the force of law. Aside from the obvious distress which may be suffered by the offending journalist, there is the question of expense for the publisher. Seeking a judicial review of the authority of a tribunal or a medical council can cost £20,000; properly representing a senior reporter who is accused of contempt may cost the equivalent of half his year's salary.

Freeing the press from any automatic obligations to disclose their sources is clearly in the public interest. Those who convey information to the media may be in no position to disclose their sources and may not even be legally entitled to do so. If a journalist could be compelled to reveal his sources, those sources would disappear and the citizenry would be afraid to blow the whistle on wrongdoing. No journalist will reveal his or her sources. To do so would mean the end of a journalistic career.

The only argument that I can see against allowing journalists to protect the confidence of sources is that an unscrupulous journalist might abuse that privilege to allow him to invent sources or to invent information and then skulk behind the cloak of legal protection. But the laws of libel and defamation clearly make such persons very vulnerable to the most awful punishment, for they place upon the journalist and the publisher the burden of proving that everything that was published was wholly true. These laws also provide the most severe penalties to be imposed on those journalists who cannot justify their stories.

Courts are very sensitive in relation to the issue of contempt. They persist in maintaining the offence of criminal contempt for those people who scandalise the court. The National Newspapers of Ireland organisation has quite correctly stated that this amounts to an attempt to cocoon the legal system and the judiciary from any criticism. Judges, of course, enjoy absolute liberty to make any and every comment on any and every matter that enters their minds when they are at work in their courts. Those who enjoy such liberties are often the last to afford similar liberties to others.

Secondly, I would like to touch on the issue of liability. In conventional actions for libel and defamation, four types of people may be held liable. They are the reporter, the editor of the newspaper or programme, the publisher and printer.

Having regard to the way modern newspapers operate, it seems to me absurd that the sanction of unlimited personal liability should attach to an ordinary reporter. The copy written by a reporter may be re-written significantly, distorted in meaning, and otherwise adjusted by people who work in newspapers before it is published. A misleading headline may be placed on top of the article written by the reporter. An incorrectly captioned picture or illustration may be appended to it. Yet the reporter may still face the most horrific legal consequences, even though he or she may have discharged his or her duty to the letter.

Similarly, it is difficult to see how a printer should be held liable for that which he prints. Modern contract printing involves the tightest possible deadlines and allows no time whatsoever for a contract printer to scrutinise that which he is printing. Newspapers invariably run late, and in order to have a newspaper on the streets in time the printer must convert camera-ready artwork into plates with the least possible delay. To expect a printer to examine the contents of the text of a newspaper within these time constraints is quite absurd.

It is quite clear to me that the only parties who should be liable in such actions are the editor of the publication and the publishing company.

I believe the laws relating to defamation are archaic and unjust. They impose an unrealistic burden of proof upon journalists and publishers. And the laws themselves lead to a narrow defensive mentality preventing proper levels of investigation and freedom of expression. Financial penalties which may be imposed on publishers, editors, reporters and printers are without limit.

Two obvious reforms which would not undermine the fairness of the system strike me as being required. It seems to me that there should be some kind of new mechanism created whereby a publisher could refer actual or threatened legal action for libel or defamation to an examining judge. That judge could then assess the degree of seriousness which ought to attach to the case. Newspapers today, whether they are national or provincial, are plagued by a litany of small claims emanating from an increasingly litigious population. Where the substance of complaint by a plaintiff is clearly trivial, it should be open to that judge at that preliminary stage to direct that claim be either struck out or settled at very modest costs.

Secondly, it should be possible for a publisher in this jurisdiction to deny liability while simultaneously making a lodgement into the courts. For six decades I think it has been possible for defendants in libel and defamation cases in the United Kingdom to make such lodgements while denying liability. In other civil actions for damages not in the area of libel and defamation in the Republic of Ireland, such a course of action is possible.

The *Sunday Business Post,* in tandem with Central Television in the United Kingdom, has begun an effort to have the rules of the upper courts altered to allow such lodgements. This case is at a reasonably advanced stage and we are heartened by the support of the Law Reform Commission for such a course of reform.

These two changes alone would create a significant improvement in the climate in which publishers operate. But they would not resolve fundamental problems afflicting those who seek to publish or broadcast. Recent Irish political history has shown that politicians were fully aware of the loaded nature of the libel law. They have been prepared to initiate actions against newspapers in the hope that they may therefore stifle all public criticism of their actions. They have claimed that they were defamed by criticisms which, in my view, amounted to nothing more than robust debating points of a non-personalised nature. To permit such intimidation of media is outrageous.

I believe that the best method of dealing with this process is to introduce a law which applies to the defamation of public figures and to matters involving public interests. In such cases, for a libel action to succeed, it should be necessary for the plaintiff to show that the publisher was actuated by malice or that the journalist involved showed a reckless disregard for the facts. This would introduce into Irish law some elements similar to those of the US law.

Lest anyone should feel that journalists are forever seeking to write a prescription which would allow them and their editors to behave in an intemperate fashion, I believe that other reforms are needed that would protect the interests of the plaintiff. In particular, I believe that it is necessary that legal aid should be available to people who have not got the resources to take an action for libel and defamation.

I would also like to turn now to the question of gagging writs. In the last two years it has become apparent that large corporations and branches of the public service use the law to gag the press. They do so in the knowledge that most newspaper proprietors dread the expense of such actions and that the plaintiff body has vastly superior resources with which to press home an action.

It costs little or nothing to serve a plenary summons on a journalist or an editor, or to oblige a solicitor to pen an entirely overblown piece of correspondence to the newspaper. For a small outlay the plaintiff can trigger a process which obliges the publisher to spend thousands of pounds in researching a defence, in briefing counsel, and in generally preparing for an action which may never materialise. Organisations which have something to hide readily embark on such claims, often urging their executives to do likewise and indemnifying those executives against legal expense. In such cases statements of claim may have to be issued and further particulars may have to be sought. Large expenses are incurred.

The process is invariably successful from the point of view of the plaintiff. The publisher tends to draw back and ceases investigating the plaintiff or his business. The executives of the plaintiff company are quizzed by other reporters or indeed by politicians and claim that the matter is *sub judice*. The matter can drag on interminably with huge expenses clocking up, and then is dropped or settled when convenient for the plaintiff.

Faced with supine editors and programme controllers, the plaintiff may even extract an apology which is then subsequently shown to be unsoundly based. And this has happened in a number of cases in the past two years.

Aside from the ease with which the wealthy and the powerful may issue proceedings for libel and defamation, there is another separate way in which the press may be gagged. This method involves the plaintiff proceeding to injunct a publisher from publishing on the grounds that the information in the possession of the publisher is confidential. The demand for injunctive relief based on either a breach of confidence or breach of copyright opens up innumerable possibilities for those who desire to suppress facts.

There is a considerable body of case law which supports such actions by plaintiffs and, in Ireland, the right to keep private information concerning publicly owned corporations was supported in the case of *ACC* v *Irish Business* magazine. It seems to me that unless there is a freedom of information act, and that unless other aspects of the law are reformed, more and more people will seek such injunctive relief based on confidentiality and copyright.

In relation to the issue of privacy, I believe that in Ireland there is no great problem with the media intruding into the private lives of ordinary or exalted citizens. Although there have been clear breaches of the unwritten code which binds Irish journalists, such as last year's publication of the most intimate details of the Eamonn Casey affair, in general the press and the broadcasters have not encroached on these sensitive areas. For that reason alone, I think it would be inadvisable for the authorities to consider systems of legal control such as those which are now proposed in the United Kingdom.

The principle of self-regulation operates quite effectively in this jurisdiction. The Postal and Telecommunications Act 1983 prohibits in this jurisdiction publication of information derived from intercepted phonecalls and even prohibits publishers from adverting to the fact that such calls have been intercepted. Last week saw the publication in full of the text of the so-called Camillagate tapes by leading broadsheet newspapers in Ireland. If the recorded conversation contained some matters of political importance, one might see some justification in publishing them. But the contents of the tapes were no more than long-distance pillow talk of a puerile nature. The decision to publish was in my view an unnecessary intrusion into the private lives of two rather silly people.

To conclude, Irish journalists operate in a difficult and dangerous legal climate. They may be threatened with jail for contempt, they may be injuncted, and they may be bankrupted by ruinous legal costs. The law as it stands offers a perfect framework for the suppression of information which should be in the public domain, a perfect framework for protecting those who wish to hide from the investigations of a free press and, as we saw last year, a perfect framework for the use of extensive litigation by public figures to muzzle the media and muzzle criticisms.

Despite, or because of, all the legal restrictions, the work of many print journalists and broadcasters in the past two years has been quite superb. Courageous investigative reporting has introduced new levels of accountability into our society. Layers have been peeled away as journalists have exposed what is really going on beneath the surface. Ultimately what counts most is the courage of the individual reporter and the courage of the person who directs that reporter.

Legal reforms may come in time, and they will indeed be welcome, but journalists will still get themselves into legal hot water. They will still be called to account before judges. They will still be pursued by grey men with long brown envelopes. That is how it should be. For the function of real journalism is not to operate in harmony with the establishment. The function of journalism is to uncover the facts that others want to hide and to publish those facts clearly and fairly. Good journalism will inevitably draw fire from the establishment. Summonses, writs, claims for injunctions, threats of imprisonment, all of these things are outward signs that the journalists have decided to do the right thing regardless of the consequences. They are our badge of honour.

Patrick MacEntee

I HAVE BEEN asked by the organisers of this conference to see to it as best I can that you go away from this conference better informed about the law. I don't know if I can do that. I shall certainly attempt to do it, but the difficulty is that the panoply of laws which make inroads on freedom of expression is so great that it will take some time. I want to approach this subject by setting out first of all what the aspirations towards freedom of expression are, because it is against those aspirations that we must measure the present state of affairs.

The first great statement of aspiration is contained in the Declaration of the Rights of Man of 26 August 1789. Article 11 of that instrument says:

The free communication of thoughts and opinions is one of the most precious of mankind's rights. Accordingly, every citizen shall be free to speak, write and publish freely, save only that he shall be answerable for the abuse of that liberty as provided by law.

There we start.

The First Amendment to the American Constitution provides, in a more succinct and even bolder way, for the same aspiration. "Congress should make no law abridging the freedom of speech or of the press." I mention the First Amendment because, while we clearly cannot go into it this morning, the American system has approached questions of freedom of information and freedom of expression, in virtually all its institutions, with greater commitment than we have – perhaps because of the clarity of the First Amendment and because of the point from which the American experience begins.

When we came to formulate our aspirations in our first Constitution, we provided that the right of free expression and opinion is guaranteed for purposes not opposed to public morality – even from the outset we're talking about public morality. The present Constitution of 1937 guarantees liberty for the exercise, subject to public order and morality, of the right of citizens to express freely their convictions and opinions, but it goes on to say:

The education of public opinion being, however, a matter of

such grave import to the common good, the State shall endeavour to ensure that organs of public opinion, such as the radio, the press, the cinema, while preserving their rightful liberty of expression, including criticism of Government policy, shall not be used to undermine public order or morality or the authority of the State.

As you see, in contrast to the first Constitution, which was concerned only to hedge about public morality, we've now introduced two new concepts: public order and the authority of the state. It continues:

The publication or utterance of blasphemous, seditious, or indecent matter is an offence which shall be punishable in accordance with law.

That's the basic document from which our laws and our institutions relating to freedom of expression come. Now, Article 19 of the United Nations Universal Declaration of Human Rights, 1948, provides that everyone has the right to freedom of opinion and expression. This includes "freedom to hold opinions without interference and to seek, receive, and impart information and ideas through any media and regardless of frontiers."

Immediately after the Second World War, the aspiration to free speech was being stated in more clear and categoric terms. However, it is right to say that Article 19 which I have just quoted from must be read together with Article 30, which provides that

Nothing in this declaration may be interpreted as implying for any state, group, or person, any right to engage in any activity or to perform any act aimed at the destruction of any of the rights and freedoms set forth therein.

So the reservations of the Universal Declaration are reasonable and sensible ones. Then we come to the European Convention on Human Rights, where it is provided by Article 10 of that convention, to which the state is a party, that

Everyone has the right of freedom of speech. His right shall include freedom to hold opinions and to receive and impart information and ideas without interference by public authority and regardless of frontiers. This Article should not prevent states from requiring the licensing of broadcasting television or cinema enterprises.

And that's fine as far as it goes. But Article 2 provides that

The exercise of these freedoms, since it carries with it duties and responsibilities, may be subject to some formalities, conditions, restrictions and penalties as are prescribed by law and are necessary in a democratic society in the interest of national security, territorial integrity or public safety for the prevention of disorder or crime, for the protection of health or morals, for the protection of the reputation and rights of others, preventing the disclosure of information received in confidence, and for maintaining the authority and impartiality of the judiciary.

If you look at the second list of reservations you will find that it is drawn to recognise the law in the states of western Europe, including England. Indeed, the English situation when the European Convention came into force largely contributed to these reservations. It is hedged about, left, right and centre.

These are aspirational documents, some of them generous, some of them extremely conditional and hedged about. What, then, is the situation in this country now, today? There is a vast panoply of statutory provisions and common law provisions which make inroads upon freedom of expression.

You have heard from the previous three speakers of their experiences of these restrictions and reservations. I shall attempt to list them in what may appear to be some tedious detail because I think it is important, in approaching a subject as fundamental as this, to know with some precision what the true situation is. Because, if we don't know what the restraints on our freedom are, then we run the risk of fighting enemies that are not there.

I now propose to set out those laws which strike me as making major inroads on freedom of expression. For reasons that will appear, it is not possible to be absolutely sure that you have got everything. Until I read Nuala O'Faolain's article in the newspaper recently I had not known that it is an offence to make nasty noises during the sermon at Mass. It is apparently. It is one of the few things I've felt inclined to do.

There may be others, skulking in the Victorian and earlier law, offences of which I am not aware, but which an ingenious Director of Public Prosecutions, or an ingenious police sergeant, will turn up in the future. We'll wait with enthusiasm to see what new gem is produced. But, to get on with the business, the most obvious point of departure for me, certainly, is the Offences Against the State Act of 1939, still in force, still daily applied, insofar as it relates to the subject.

Section 10 of that act provides that it is an offence
to set up in type, print, publish, send out through the post, distribute, sell or offer for sale, any document which is, or contains, or includes, an incriminating document, which is, or contains, or includes, a treasonable document, or is, or contains, or includes, a seditious document.

What then are these incriminating documents, treasonable documents and seditious documents? They are defined, as in the case of incriminating documents, "a document of whatsoever date, or bearing no date, issued by or emanating from any unlawful organisation or appearing to be issued or so to emanate, or appearing to aid or abet any such organisation or calculated to promote the formation of an unlawful organisation." A treasonable document is defined as "including a document alleged to lead directly or indirectly to the commission of treason".

The expression "seditious document" includes "a document consisting of, or containing matter calculated to, or attempting to, undermine the public order or the authority of the state", and "a document that alleges, implies, or suggests, or is calculated to suggest, that the government functioning under the Constitution is not the lawful government of the state and that there is in existence in the state any body or organisation not functioning under the government which is entitled to be recognised as the government of the country." Also included in the definition is "a document which alleges, implies, or suggests, or is calculated to do that, that military forces maintained under the Constitution are not the lawful military forces of the state, or a document in which words or abbreviations, or symbols, refer to a military body or are used in referring to an unlawful organisation."

Section 10 of that act provides that
Any person who sends or contributes to any newspaper, or other periodical publication, or for the proprietor of any newspaper or other periodical publication publishing such newspaper or publication, any letter, article or communication which was sent, or contributed, or purported to be sent or contributed to on behalf of an unlawful organisation shall be a contravention of that section.

And there are then provisions requiring printers of documents to keep copies so that they may be examined by the Guards, and to publish the name of the printer and the author on all documents, and to keep them and to allow the Guards to enter premises for the purpose of examining them. As if that was not adequate to see to that area, the Offences Against the State (Amendment) Act 1972 in Section 4.1 provides that

Any public statement made orally, in writing, or otherwise, that constitutes an interference with the course of justice shall be unlawful, and the statement shall be deemed to constitute an interference with the course of justice if it is intended or is of such a character as to be likely, directly or indirectly, to influence any court, person or authority concerned with the institution, conduct, or defence of any civil or criminal proceeding, including a party or witness, as to whether or how he should proceed, should institute, conduct, continue, or defend, or as to what should be the outcome of the criminal proceedings.

So, the Offences Against the State Act then, in the area to which it relates, has enormous powers of control and censorship of information. Very widespread, so widespread that the government of South Africa is alleged to have resorted to it as a model for certain restrictive legislation in that jurisdiction. Now, draconian though the Offences Against the State Act undoubtedly is, the act has no machinery for censorship of newspapers. It can only proceed by way of prosecution after the event.

However, it is otherwise in relation to the broadcasting media. Under the Broadcasting Authority Acts of 1960 and 1976 the RTE Authority is subject to the directives of the Minister for Communications. And if the minister is of the opinion that the broadcasting of particular matter, or of any matter of a particular class, would be likely to promote or incite crime or tend to undermine the authority of the state, he may, by order, direct the authority to refrain from broadcasting the matter, or any matter of a particular class, and the Authority is obliged to comply with that prohibition.

That order remains in force for a maximum period of 12 months, but may be renewed and extended for further periods of a maximum 12 months, and under the provisions of the Radio and Television Act of 1988, all such orders are binding on independent radio and television companies. So there you have the possibility of actual censorship.

There are two cases in which it has been established that decisions to prohibit and decisions in relation to the application of prohibition orders are capable of being reviewed in the courts, and one decision, that of Mr Justice O'Hanlon in *O'Toole v RTE*, indicates that, for once, the courts are disposed to look at the application of Section 31 of the Broadcasting Act in a way that favours freedom of expression.

One understands that Michael D. Higgins, who is now in charge of this area of the law, is no great admirer of Section 31, but he has been advised that the order presently in existence cannot be abrogated and must be allowed to run its course. I'm not in a position to express any very strong view as to whether there is a way round that, but, one way or the other, one might reasonably hope that when the currency of the present Section 31 order runs its course, it will not be renewed.

The next great area of inroads on freedom of expression is the Official Secrets Act of 1963. Section 4 of that Act provides

that a person should not communicate any official information to any other person unless he is duly authorised to do so, or does so in the course of and in accordance with his duties as the holder of a public office and when it is his duty in the interest of the state to communicate it.

Section 5(1) provides

that a person who is or has been a party to a contract with a Minister, or state authority, or any person on behalf of the Minister, or state authority, or is employed by that party shall not communicate to any third party any information related to the contract or expressed therein to be confidential.

Section 9 provides

that a person should not, in any manner prejudicial to the safety or preservation of the state obtain, report, communicate to any other person or publish, or have in his possession or under his control any document containing, or other record whatsoever containing, or other record whatsoever of information relating to the Army, the Garda Síochána or any other matter whatsoever confirmation as to which would or might be prejudicial to the safety or preservation of the state.

But, reasonable as it may appear to be on the face of it, the Official Secrets Act is an Alice in Wonderland because, while it turns on the definition of what is official information, it provides that official information is what the minister says it is. If the minister says it's official information, then it is official information, and that is that. The act is so broadly drawn that any document concerning the public service can be said to be an official document by the minister and therefore *is* an official document.

The Ponting case in England, of course, has compelled the English to look anew at their Official Secrets Act, and there is a strong case for saying that this is one of the acts that should be looked at urgently and immediately and restricted in its operation.

Even an apparently benign act like the National Archives Act of 1988 gives rise to problems. Under this act there is a general right to inspect departmental records over 30 years old. However, this general right is ousted where an authorised officer certifies that to make specific material available for public inspection would be contrary to the public interest. The term "contrary to the public interest" is not defined, and while, in theory, an arbitrary exclusion might be reviewed by the courts, this is hardly an adequate remedy when what you want is access to material to see what it is in the first place.

It's very hard to see how you can effectively go to court and say "I've been excluded from something I ought to have access to" if you've never been allowed near it in the first place and can't know whether it is or isn't – and this, of course, in the context of the fact that any legal proceedings, either by way of judicial review, or anything else, are costly.

Several semi-state institutions and organisations such as the IDA and the Central Bank have in their founding statutes provisions requiring rigorous confidentiality by officers and employees analogous to those in the Official Secrets Act. I would suggest that all such provisions should be looked at anew, urgently, with a view to reducing the scope of the secrecy and suppression of freedom of expression, and keeping it to the absolute minimum necessary to allow these and similar institutions to do their job. We need to see to it that the confidentiality provisions are not such as can be used to stop bona fide discussion of incompetence, poor work practices or simple differences of opinion about decisions.

Ireland does not have a freedom of information act. Nor does it seem to be on the way to having one. This again is a matter that it should not be impossible to get our government to consider, and to consider as a matter of urgency. America has opened up – not as far as it should have, and not without difficulty – official information. Several states in western Europe have, and we need to do so and we need to do it urgently.

I want then to pass briefly and refer to Ireland's passion for censorship. One of the things that we seem to be committed to, and passionate about, is censoring. We started off with the common law position for a number of years after the state was founded whereby obscene matter was dealt with as a common law misdemeanour, that of obscenity. But very soon, when we got into our stride in 1929 we got into the censorship business in a big way. And we renewed our censorship law in 1949, and we have, thank heavens, modified it somewhat since then, but it is still a serious weapon in the armoury of those who are not enthusiastic about freedom of expression.

The 1949 act established a Censorship Board consisting of five persons appointed by the Minister for Justice. No qualifications are required, although I suppose literacy is implied. They were empowered to make prohibition orders in respect of books and periodicals.

The board might take on the task of considering a book on its own initiative – although how do they do that, when you think about it? Do they go to the local shop and look for dirty books? I don't know. But they can do it on their own initiative, or they can receive complaints from members of the public. (I once complained to the Censorship of Publications Board: I sent them a copy of *Peter Pan,* in which there is a passage of very considerable obscenity if you can only spot it. I even underlined it in blue.) Or they can consider books that have been seized by the Customs on importation. Now, the board is required to consider whether a prohibition order should be made in regard to a particular book, and the board is required to take into account the literary, artistic, scientific, historical merit or importance of the book, the general tenor of the book, the language in which it is written – I'm not sure what that means: the language in the sense of English or Irish, or whether it means the style – the nature and extent of the circulation which in the board's opinion may be reasonably expected to read it. The sentence seems to leave a little bit to be desired, as well as the thought. I suppose it means, I hope it means, whether it's children or adults. Perhaps it means whether you should let your servants read it.

The board may communicate with the author, editor, or publisher and may take his representations into account. The vital question of whether an Irish Family Planning Association pamphlet should have been banned or not was successfully left unresolved because the court decided the case on the basis that the IFPA board should have been communicated with, could have been communicated with, and were not communicated with, and thus avoided answering the question as to whether the censoring of family planning information was constitutional.

In any event, the board having duly examined the book with those criteria in mind may form the opinion that it is indecent or obscene, or, and this I think is the really significant part of the censorship mechanism, that it "advocates the unnatural prevention of conception or the procurement of abortion or miscarriage, or the use of any method, treatment or appliance for the purpose of such prevention or procurement, or for any of those reasons," sale or distribution in the state, should be prohibited. If the board reaches such a conclusion it is required to prohibit publications.

Then there are provisions in relation to periodicals which are based on past performance and can procure the prohibition of a periodical in the future. There is a board of appeal, and more recent legislation has provided for a review of censorship orders made before a certain date, or where they were made a certain period of time ago. They're no longer perpetual. They were. But now an author or publisher can make a new application after a period of time.

The Censorship Appeals Board has a judge as its chairman, and one can appeal from the original Censorship of Publications Board to that Appeals Board. The effective period of prohibition under the 1967 (Amendment) Act is now 12 years. You can try again after that. In recent years there have been fewer, but still some prohibition orders affecting serious works.

However, it seems to me that the seriousness of censorship has been its chilling effect upon the perfectly legitimate, indeed necessary, debates about contraception and abortion. Also, you will recall, we recently banned – or the Censorship of Publications Board did on our behalf – the Madonna book. They undoubtedly achieved the very opposite of what they set out to achieve there. Is that sort of thing necessary in a mature society?

Film censorship is carried on under the Censorship of Films Acts of 1923 and 1970 – and is done not by a board but by a film censor. Again, the 1970 (Amendment) Act does more or less the same thing as the Censorship of Publications Act by allowing orders originally permanent in nature to expire, or it allows application to be made after seven years.

We have now given ourselves a Video Recording Act which establishes the office of official censor, and he has powers even more extensive than the film censor in that his criteria are wider – a new addition to our panoply of censoring mechanisms. He can refuse a certificate if he feels that, on viewing the film, it would be "likely to cause a person to commit crimes whether by inciting or encouraging them to do so, or by indicating or suggesting ways of doing so, or of avoiding detection." Or, if he thinks that the film would be "likely to stir up hatred against persons, in the state or elsewhere, on account of their race, colour, nationality, religious, ethnic or national origins, membership of the travelling community, or sexual orientation, or would tend by reason of the inclusion in it of obscene or indecent matter to deprave or corrupt persons who might view it." Or "if it depicts acts of gross violence or gross cruelty including mutilation or torture towards human beings or animals".

Well, ladies and gentlemen, I have set out the censorship statutes, but it does not follow from that that I am arguing, or that one can validly argue, that all censorship must go, although I know there are those who believe that. What I am asking for is that there should be a close examination of every statute that makes inroads on freedom of expression. That it is either got out of the way totally, if it is unnecessary, or, if it is deemed to be necessary, that its scope should be confined to its legitimate, proper purposes, and that there should not be an overspill which kills proper, legitimate communication and debate which is fundamental to a democratic society.

The other two major areas which are chilling, very chilling in some cases, as we heard from Steve MacDonogh, of freedom of expression, are the areas of defamation law and the area of the contempt of court. A book could be written on either of these subjects. In relation to defamation I agree with every word that Steve MacDonogh has said. However, I think it is important to say that the Law Reform Commission has made a number of very important suggestions for law reform in this area. I understand that the election manifesto of the Labour Party backed those law reform recommendations or the bulk of them. I have been unable to find any similar commitment in the Programme for Government. That seems to be sad. One hopes it is an oversight and perhaps one of the things that we can see in this conference is whether it is an oversight, because if it is an oversight, it's a very serious oversight.

Specifically the Law Reform Commission has suggested a device to deal with the problem of gagging writs. The device proposed is not, in my view, adequate because its timescale is too long. It may be the best that is constitutionally permissible. But my own view is that the best way to deal with the problem of gagging writs is to appoint enough judges and court officials to see that libel actions can be dealt with promptly because freedom of expression is important. People's reputations are at risk, and it's not an area where delay can be countenanced. And I believe that if actions for defamation could be got on with sufficient promptness, the problem of gagging writs would, to a large extent, go away.

The other important recommendation is that it should be possible to bring an action for a declaratory judgement, that is to say for a statement from the court that what was said about you was wrong, was false and was defamatory. It would not be an action for damages but it would be an action that would allow the courts to order a retraction, a correction and an apology. That certainly would go some of the way to speeding the operations up and keeping the balance between reputation and freedom.

There is also a recommendation that there would be a defence in certain circumstances in an action for defamation where the defendant shows that the words complained of were comment and that the comments were supported by facts, but that there were insufficient facts to support the comment. The defendant would not necessarily lose his action provided he exercised reasonable care in ascertaining the truth of the facts alleged in support of the comment. The commission recommends that in those circumstances the plaintiff should not be entitled to general damages, but would be entitled to special damages and to a correction order and a declaratory order.

These proposed reforms are important. Of course they would not go far enough to meet all the difficulties that the press have, but they would be part of a course of redress, and they might in due course be consolidated.

I do not feel that there is time to deal with the question of contempt of court adequately and I think it's perhaps best left.

Damien Kiberd has referred to it and it is a very real problem. Here again there are some hopeful signs. In a recent judgement in the High Court, O'Hanlon J. declined to follow the generally accepted restrictive view of the law of contempt and preferred to follow the more liberal jurisprudence of the European Court of Human Rights at Strasbourg.

It is obvious that I have not been comprehensive. There is the question of cabinet confidentiality. There is a black hole into which nobody can look at all. There cannot be light there; the Supreme Court has said so. We are now faced with a legal argument that that black hole should have a fellow black hole beside it to cover Dáil confidentiality.

There is the new risk to anyone who says anything about anything, that you'll end up before a tribunal of inquiry paying expensive barristers and having your life disrupted and not being able to go to certain pubs. But I think I've said enough to indicate that there is a vast array of weapons in the armoury of those who are not enthusiastic for free exchange of information.

Ladies and gentlemen, the day before yesterday, a friend of mine told me a story. A story about a conference on freedom of expression very much like this one – of course, not this one – where the organisers had thought it would be a very nice idea to invite a talented young actor along to put on a small performance illustrative of the difficulties of those who would have freedom of expression in the face of those who would not. And apparently this young man suggested to the organisers that he would perform one of the great set speeches from Brian Friel's *Freedom of the City*. The organisers thought about this proposal and told him, no. It's not acceptable. It's too republican. Think about it.

CENSORSHIP AND THE ARTS

Luke Gibbons

In September 1978 the then Editor-in-Chief of the *Observer*, Conor Cruise O'Brien, registered his strong objections to the publication of an article in the *Observer Magazine* by Mary Holland. The article dealt with the increasing polarisation of the nationalist community in Northern Ireland, using as an illustration the case history of a working-class Derry woman, Mary Neelis. The story is similar to that of a Sikh woman in the aftermath of the assassination of Indira Ghandi cited by Salman Rushdie; Indian television at the time went to extraordinary lengths to prevent this woman speaking on television. Conor Cruise O'Brien's objections to the Holland article are instructive; he argued that it elicited sympathy by portraying her as a victim of the troubles. Yet Mary Neelis had three sons serving sentences for offences committed in the service of the IRA. This of itself should not have placed her in the dock, but in Ireland things are not quite like this. O'Brien explained:

> Since Irish republicanism, especially the killing strain, has a very high propensity to run in families, and since the mother is most often the carrier, I incline to the view that a mother whose sons behave in this way had something to do with what they believe and how they behave.

It is as if motherhood itself is an offence.

The mother and the maternal body have often figured as allegories of Ireland by writers, poets and dramatists over the past centuries. But the mother and the maternal body are not allegorical figures; rather, they are quite literally vehicles of the nation. Actual women are the republican tradition. Allegories and artistic figures have become part of reality; the representations themselves have become real. It is no wonder O'Brien went to such lengths to control not just media representations but other cultural forms such as popular ballads. Popular culture in the widest sense of the word is people speaking about their experiences in their own voices, in a public sphere. That this is an underlying source of O'Brien's anxiety is clear from something else in the letter to Mary Holland:

> You are a very poor judge of Irish Catholics. That gifted and talkative community includes some of the most expert conmen and conwomen in the world, and in this case I believe you have been conned.

This is another representation taking on material form. In fact, it is one of the oldest colonial stereotypes of the Irish: that as actors they are wily, loquacious, possessing the gift of the gab with a natural talent for lying and dissimulation. In other words, Irish people are acting all the time. Theatre is out in the streets. Theatre is in every community. We are dissimulating all the time; the representation becomes real and the gap between the theatrical and the real is blurred and obscured.

The desire to police the maternal body in O'Brien's remarks reveals an important link between gender and politics in Ireland. There is no distinction between the public and the private in Irish social life. The areas of experience which lend themselves conventionally to the novel and other forms of imaginative representation, in other words human relationships and the family, are what Carl Bernstein referred to as the texture of everyday life. These are the kinds of areas with which writers, painters and imaginative representations deal. "The bits and pieces of everyday life," as Patrick Kavanagh said. But these are already charged with politics in Ireland. It's as if even these areas are charged with political significance. This helps to explain why Gerry Adams's seemingly apolitical short stories or reminiscences are in some ways considered more lethal than his expressed political statements, and why a pronouncement by Sinn Féin about mushroom growing in Ireland is not above suspicion. Everything is politicised according to this logic. The fact that ordinary life itself is a site of conflict draws together unwittingly two of the most powerful forms of censorship in Ireland: Section 31 and the Orwellian attempts to control both information and first-hand accounts of women's experiences during the abortion and divorce referenda.

Both of these prohibitions work on the assumption that nothing is so dangerous as the voice from below. The victims of discrimination or oppression relate their own first-hand experience with the minimum media packaging of the product. It is no coincidence that oral delivery and the voice itself carries this suspicion with regard to representations in Ireland, as if the very grain of the voice somehow disturbs the equilibrium of society.

The profound distrust of the grain of the voice was nowhere more evident than during the abortion and the divorce campaigns in Ireland in the 1980s, when media coverage of issues was restricted to so-called experts, media professionals and public figures within the tightly-organised, closed formats of current affairs programmes. The current affairs programme, the high ground of politics, was chosen as the format to discuss sexual politics and the family – areas that in other cultures would be seen as belonging to the private domain and private morality. In Ireland, however, the public and the private cross over, quarantined within the rigidly-organised format and artificial discussion of current affairs programmes in contrast to the open-ended spontaneous discussions of phone-in programmes or talk-shows. Rather than being the opium of the masses as described by Bernstein, talk-shows and phone-in programmes in Ireland provided unscripted, relatively spontaneous access to broadcasting, where women spoke for the first time in the public sphere. Other formats were expressly forbidden from dealing with abortion and divorce; the *Late Late Show* was absurdly turned into a legal forum with this spurious idea of balance and objectivity. There was not a woman in sight to register or talk about her experience in her own voice. This is what I mean by the confiscation of the voice.

While one form of censorship directly intervenes in people's lives, there's another more subtle form of censorship which has to do with agenda setting. Certain people get access to the airwaves, to publishing, to film or whatever. They represent other people, but the people who are represented never get to represent themselves. The function of art is not simply to represent people but to empower people, to make people agents of their own representations. Throughout the various forms of state intervention, the voice and the reader from below are really anathema to intellectual and cultural debate. This constitutes a far wider form of control of access than simple direct state intervention. The Censorship of Publications Act 1929 applied to the social class of reader; hardcover books were not censored, but paperbacks, which were read by the working class, were. This subaltern culture is one where people are represented but cannot represent themselves. This is one of the main issues raised by representation and agency in the arts.

Robert Ballagh

AT THE OUTSET many of you might be inclined to think that the issue of censorship and the visual arts simply does not arise. After all, in Ireland and in most countries with which we are familiar, there are very few examples of paintings being censored and fewer still of artists being banned. However, in the visual arts such an observation proves absolutely nothing, for the world of the visual arts is entirely different to that of any other art form in one crucial and fundamental way. The principal motivation behind the censorship of art, by any establishment, is to prevent the general public from having access to any ideas that might subvert the authority of that establishment. The banning of artists is usually intended as punishment against whoever dares to challenge that authority.

In Ireland we are very familiar with these procedures. We have a long history of denial of public access to information, artistic or otherwise. One of the first legislative acts adopted by the Irish Free State was the Censorship of Films Act 1924. This was followed quickly by the Censorship of Publications Act 1929. The early method of book censorship illustrates the patronising attitude of the establishment in its desire to exercise control over the general public. Many books banned in paperback could be obtained quite easily in hardback. It was obviously believed that those who could afford to purchase hardbacks were to be trusted.

These examples indicate that the real purpose of artistic censorship is to break any possible connection that a challenging artist might forge with the general public. Yet, when we examine the visual arts, we quickly discover that such an analysis is irrelevant; as far as contemporary visual arts are concerned, there is no general public. Tom Wolfe, the American author, put it most succinctly in his essay "The Painted Word":

The notion that the public accepts or rejects anything in modern art, the notion that the public scorns, ignores, fails to comprehend, allows to wither, crushes the spirit of, or commits any other crime against art or any individual artist is merely a romantic fiction, a bitter-sweet trilby sentiment. The public plays no part in the process whatsoever. The public is not invited. The game is completed and the trophies distributed long before the public knows what has happened. The public that buys books in hardcover and paperback by the millions. The public that buys records by the billions and fills stadiums for concerts. The public that spends a million dollars on a single movie, this public affects taste, theory and artistic outlook in literature, music and drama, even though courtly elites hang on somewhat desperately in each field. The same has never been true in art. The public whose glorious numbers are recorded in the annual reports of the museums, all those students and bus tours and mums and dads and random intellectuals are merely tourists, autograph seekers, gawkers, parade watchers. As far as deciding which artist will be successful or which style will be in vogue the public is presented with a *fait accompli*.

The artist moved from being literally the house guest of the nobility to a semi-detached situation, where the artist was an invited participant in intellectual salons organised by the 18th century bourgeoisie, to finally becoming the alienated bohemian artist of the 19th century. In the course of this historical journey to modern artist, the role and audience for the artist's work altered quite radically. In the past, artists like Leonardo da Vinci and Michelangelo saw nothing unusual in painting what they were told. What they painted fitted quite comfortably into the social and the religious fabric of their time. However, the situation has changed since the 19th century. Artists work quite independently now, painting for themselves with no specific audience in mind. Paradoxically, the actual consumer of contemporary art is quite specific and belongs to what Tom Wolfe referred to as *le monde* in "The Painted Word".

This consists of the milieu of those who find it important to be in fashion, the orbit of aristocrats, wealthy bourgeois, publishers, writers, journalists, impresarios, performers who wish to be where things happen... But what about *le monde*, the culturati, the social members of the set; what's in it for them? Part of their reward is the ancient and semi-sacred status of benefactor of the Arts. The Arts have always been a doorway into society and in the larger cities today, the Arts, the museum boards, Arts Councils, fun drives, openings, parties, committee meetings have completely replaced the churches in this respect. But there is more. Today there is a particularly modern reward that the avant garde artist can give his benefactor. Namely, the feeling that he, like his mate, the artist, is separate from and aloof from the bourgeoisie, the middle classes; the feeling that he is from the middle class but he is no longer in it. The feeling that he is a fellow soldier or at least an aide-de-camp in the vanguard march through the land of the Philistines.

The end result is that the vast majority of contemporary artists make art works that are consciously self-indulgent and quite defiant of public taste. Together with a small public – necessarily small, for few in society are wealthy enough to purchase original art works – their main interest in art is motivated by a desire to express its separateness from the great unwashed through the appreciation and purchase of so-called difficult art works. And both the artists and "culturati" are catered for by the gallery system, which again can safely ignore the fickleness of public taste as long as a few of the initiated are prepared to purchase work that is put on display. If one was cynical, one could say that we now have arrived at a situation where the main criteria for most modernist art is that it is totally inaccessible to the general public. And this incomprehensibility in turn has spawned a legion of mediators whose main task would appear to be explaining the unexplainable. Unfortunately, to my mind, most art critics have developed a language that is just as inaccessible as the art works under question and, in essence, they have become accessories after the fact. The unconscious consensus that has developed between the artist, the *aficionado*, the gallery and the critic has created the very strong impression that real art only takes place within the privileged circle. Funding authorities certainly accept this; by checking the facts and figures, you will quickly discover that practically all funding for the visual arts goes to activities organised within that circle. Community arts – and by this I mean art generated at community level – receive almost no funding; nevertheless, an art approach that is entirely marginal to society at large is perceived as mainstream and is funded accordingly.

The resistance to art activities outside this privileged circle is more extensive than simply a refusal to fund. In my experience, community arts projects like murals and workshops, exhibitions and events in non-kosher locations like the suburbs or even department stores are simply ignored by the art establishment. The mullahs of modern ideology are not prepared to allow any artistic life outside the privileged circle; the capacity for subversion by the radical artists is extremely limited.

To illustrate this point, I will tell you a short story about a Latin American artist who some years ago painted a picture in which he wanted to expose the plight of the exploited peasants. He painted a large picture of a landowner on a horse riding through the cane fields whipping the peasants with a rather large bull-whip. The painting was very well received in an exhibition; in fact, he won a gold medal for his efforts. It was purchased by a leading collector, whom the artist was asked, at the opening of the exhibition, if he wanted to meet. The artist agreed, thanked the collector for purchasing his work and hoped that he liked the work. To which the collector replied, "It's a wonderful painting. In fact that's exactly how those bastards should be treated."

At the beginning of this short talk, I noted that formal censorship in the visual arts is practically non-existent. At this point, I hope I have shown why formal censorship is in fact unnecessary. The visual arts have moved so far to society's margins that they pose no more of a threat to the status quo than lepidopterology or philately. The world of the visual arts is controlled in such a way that even challenging ideas have little impact on society at large. This hermetic containment is enough to deny both access and participation to the general public. After attacking the paucity of most socialist realism, Che Guevara in his essay "Man and Socialism in Cuba" warned against the so-called freedom of the artist in the West:

If the rules of the game are respected all honours are obtained. The honours that might be granted are the honours that might be granted to a pirouetting monkey; the condition is not attempting to escape from the invisible cage.

Neil Belton

IN IRELAND CENSORSHIP makes a difference to peoples' lives, women's especially. It is illegal, as everyone here knows, to publish information about abortion or where it can be obtained, and for a while last year a woman was criminalised for trying to go to England to have an abortion. Young women desperate for the right to control their reproduction are the victims we can all support – the good face of silence.

It has another face in Ireland, too: that of the militant nationalist willing to plant bombs, to kill soldiers, to murder Protestant workers and to maim children for behaviour that the state would punish with a month in prison. This is a harder face, and it is hard for some of us to accept that that face has a right to be seen on Irish television. But the defenders of sectarian violence have to be seen, so that all political agents can be confronted with the consequences of their actions, and criticised for them. If you claim the right to speak, you give up the right to silence. This is a bigger problem for the IRA, in the long run, than for us.

Yet even with these restrictions, Ireland allows, on the world-scale, remarkable freedom of speech. You can say or write almost anything, transgress – at least in print – almost any taboo. Elsewhere you are more constrained. Salman Rushdie has spent four years under armed guard because he offended a theocratic dictatorship. In the Arab world, your words can kill you. To take just one recent example, the Islamic democrat Faraq Foda was shot down in Cairo for defending the Coptic Christian victims of the Muslim Brothers. The American scholar and poet Raymond Stock, a friend of Foda's, gave a concise summary of the balance between life and death, survival and expression: "He died just for what he said and wrote; he owned neither public office nor a gun." Foda's books have now been banned in Egypt. Stock is writing the life of the Nobel-Prize laureate Naguib Mahfouz, and reported recently that Mahfouz himself – Egypt's great twentieth century writer – has been sentenced to death in a *fatwa* of the Muslim Brothers. These are not tendencies unique to Islam: in the Balkans, to be a Muslim writer in a town taken by Serbian forces can be a sentence of death.

But I don't want to talk about the horrific realities out there, in case it makes us feel comfortable in here. Violence is not the only cause of silence. Both censorship and murder require conscious thought. I thought it would be useful to talk about publishing in our society, about the stories that do not get told because people do not think, and the stories that are told but not heard because the people who relay them do not think that they are important enough to amplify. And beyond that there are social forces that seem to have nothing to do with language, but which create areas of silence, and other spaces where everything becomes audible and sayable.

Take the shaping of cities in the past fifteen years: the hardening contrast between the "inner city" of buses, council flats, plastic bags and dirt, and the outer rings of houses and gardens, cars and spotless malls. The pattern is at its most extreme in the USA, with Detroit as the most frightening example of social apartheid, but there are versions of it everywhere now. It is in these twin cities that the books we publish get sold. Bookshops are in the renovated hearts of cities, expanding the middle-class market for reading through chain-owned department stores of high culture. They are the Harrods of the mind. Outside the West Ends, bookshops cannot survive or compete; libraries close; schools decline; workplaces close. Believing that books have anything to do with you, anything to say to you, becomes a matter of social geography.

It is not a matter of absolute deprivation. Ambitious poor kids can read, and fight their way into the world of culture as they have always done. But the emergence of genius from adversity is comforting only to social Darwinists. We are conditioned by the maps of our cities that we carry in our heads. The restless can cross borders, but most people do not. There are more books, more films, more forms of music in circulation than ever before, but this mass of information is saturating societies in which cultural and social frontiers are going up rather than coming down. The electronic opiates of the new entertainment industry, the repetitive games and formula videos, are backed by a vast amount of marketing money and targeted at a predominantly deskilled population. In the "inner cities", the huge video store is often the most important cultural resource – and it is located up the road from the shell of the municipal library, its budget cut along with its local authority's: starved of books and a warm place for the homeless to sleep.

Jeremiahs and elitists of all descriptions, from Matthew Arnold to Saul Bellow, from Theodor Adorno to Tom Wolfe, have been predicting for over a century that the masses will become zombies through absorbing mass culture, and they have been wrong. Creative voices continue to emerge. The Harlems and the Hackneys produce music, poetry, and drama of great energy and variety. But with the erosion of assumptions of equality, in education especially, there comes also a restriction of culture, of information, of the tools an active citizen needs to judge and criticise his or her state. The exclusion and silence of millions of citizens never reading extensively, never voting, never mattering, is a huge threat to all but the narrowest form of democracy. The questions Who reads? Who writes? are, therefore, inescapably political and constitutional. They are about the right of access, the right to a public voice.

If access to information is uneven now, consider the implications of a world in which information is available through, but also dependent on, computer networks. These "libraries without walls" will in theory make it possible to gain entry to a mass of electronic documents (journals, papers and data in digital form) by lifting a phone and connecting it to your personal computer; provided, that is, you have both of these items – no small proviso in many parts of the world today – and can pay for your subscription to the global database. Brian Perry, Director of Research at the British Library, acknowledges that "the nightmare is where a lot of the material is only available in machine-readable form". The democratic and intellectual potential of this world library – the dream of Babel restored – is truly enormous, but it may be subverted by a tighter and tighter circulation of denser and denser masses of information through the same circuits: great universities, research networks, governments and armies. Those outside the unfettered simultaneity of the high-speed conversation can talk to themselves.

The printed word, however, still occupies a central place in our culture, despite the richness of other kinds of representation in our imaginative lives. How a writer becomes an author, and writing becomes a book, are processes of unusual political importance. In the first place, companies publish for a market, and most books don't make money. Every company is under pressure to find books that will sell a great many copies to a public whose tastes are formed to a considerable extent by television and film; small companies are under huge pressure. They become part of conglomerates, and half a dozen of these dominate English language publishing. Within these empires, the temptation is to concentrate money on lines of least resistance. We live in a very mobile, fantastic world, and it is inevitable that people will want to read fantasies of escape, fulfilment and revenge. There is nothing wrong with this. But if the companies that share out most of a marketplace have too exclusive an obsession with finding and polishing new variations of the same basic narrative, the original and obstinate qualities of live writing may be overlooked.

Publishing conglomerates have other effects. Dominating the distribution of books in these islands as they do, and selling to a few large chains of bookstores, they leave little room for surprises. It is very rare for a small publisher to have a bestseller: the problems of distribution and sale are too daunting. Nothing succeeds unless a big company says it must. In other European countries, such as Germany, oligopoly is less powerful. Strong regional economies and identities, devolved political institutions and more democratic distribution systems combine to preserve markets for independent bookstores and smaller "local" publishers (who often do not think of themselves as local at all, but simply as being located in a particular place). They can be *publish*-ers, winning national audiences for some of their books, rather than – as in the British domain - semi-amateur "privishers".

I do not want to give the impression that life in a publishing conglomerate is an Orwellian existence, and that you cannot publish good, wonderful, beautiful books in the niches that these companies often deliberately create. Most of the good new books that you and I have read in the past year have probably been published by Engulf and Devour Ltd: Pan, Penguin, Random House, Bantam. Because there is at least a conventional commitment to diversity and novelty in publishing, editors can be sensitive to movements in the wider culture, and provoke important debates with the books they sponsor. But the insidious effects of a standardisation of categories – which also means a standardisation of styles and voices – have to be struggled against. You can make a lot of money by giving up that struggle: "If the public wants serial killers, we'll give 'em serial killers," as the head of a successful house said recently. This is the Hobbesian version of publishing democracy.

Where you are a publisher matters more than it should: geography again. The concentration of publishers in a single metropolitan centre, London, has the effect of creating a particular vision of what is acceptable on the periphery. For example, Irish *authors* are successful when they are selected by cosmopolitan London publishers; Irish *publishers* are successful when they stick to books of Irish interest. Our provincialism is a story not entirely of our own scripting.

The restriction of possibilities can also occur at the most intimate human level, in the guts of individual taste. The choice of books for publication, the transformation of quantity into quality that happens when you can call yourself an "author", has been made for over a century by editors and "readers". These watchdogs at the gates of print have themselves been drawn from a stratum that makes the upper reaches of the British civil service look democratic. Indeed the mandarin system in Whitehall *is* more democratic because it is roughly based on merit, whereas the editors of literary London have relied on a network of talent, good taste and flair – as well as social connections, nepotism and the blinkers of one kind of cultural tradition. Oxford and Cambridge rule, to a staggering extent, even after fifteen years of supposedly corrosive social mobility and thirty years before that of social-democratic egalitarianism.

I suggested earlier that reading and writing lead you quickly into politics. My personal view is that publishing in Britain – which determines the fate of Irish writers too – reflects, like most British institutions, the archaic British state in its nostalgia, its delusions of world power status, its social narrowness and its xenophobia. It would already be a disastrous provincial sink, a cultural Austria, if it had not been for the contributions of exiled European Jews and immigrants from the Commonwealth. Deutsch, Weidenfeld, Maschler and Warburg knew about a wider world, and it took an Irish-Lebanese-Australian woman to set up Virago and reveal a huge reading public of liberated women. Yet some of the absences are still striking. Irish literature has played a certain role in the formation of the modern English canon, yet in the midst of a minor Irish literary revival there are perhaps three Irish editors with any power in London publishing. There is *one* "black" person in an editorial position.

Let me give one further example of the way in which the strange atmosphere of the British legal and political state, in which individuals are "subjects" and not "citizens", seeps into this business of getting out books. Notoriously, British industry is saddled with an elite of highly paid managers drawn from the usual schools and colleges. Their inability to halt the decline of the economy is matched only by their facility in the art of managerial rhetoric, and their slavish loyalty to a politics that has destroyed the industrial base and much of the infrastructure of their country without replacing it with anything more creative. One of the key features of this social group (there are great exceptions, of course, but the general tendency seems undeniable) is its insulation from the business of production. This has very deep cultural roots, and the visible apex of the phenomenon is the scramble for the honours list: like the *Hofrats* and *Ritters* of late Habsburg Austria, these are bourgeois ashamed of their status, drawn to the glamour of the monarchy and its orders.

In publishing, this deferential tradition fosters a lack of respect for those who remain engaged with texts and authors; a subtle downgrading of editorial skills, so that more and more of the actual work is farmed out to freelancers paid by the hour; a cult of the editor as purchaser, but not active assistant in the creation of books; and an enormous reliance on agents as the real source of new ideas and authors. The decline in standards that must be apparent to anyone who compares books published in the USA with those produced in London, is caused by deep historical currents in the flow of national life.

The set of harmonious loose arrangements that makes up the culture of British publishing – uncoerced, undogmatic, working reasonably well, not formally very democratic but allowing a diversity of opinion – could, as I have said, be the literary mirror of the unwritten English constitution. I am sorry if this sounds totalising, but it is hard to separate out the economic, political and cultural effects of what is now widely seen to be a real crisis of the British polity. The half-modern, half-feudal twilight makes the English South look like the centre of the world, and writing from the English North or Scotland or Wales look rough, minor, and marginal or poetic, visionary, Celtic and fantastic. It depends on its degree of distance from the established norm. African or Latin American writing is radiant, in this optic, with the colours of exoticism: dazzling yet somehow invisible. One of the deepest unplumbed assumptions of people who live inside this world is the centrality of the literary itself. Literature as the central expression of the culture, the best essence of Englishness. (It is interesting that the cultural critics who have attacked this dominance of Eng. Lit. most forcefully have been Irish or Scottish – Perry Anderson, Francis Mulhern and Tom Nairn – or Afro-Caribbean, like Stuart Hall.) Traditional forms of fiction, poetry and reminiscence are privileged massively. The weekly literary pages are the rock-beds where these attitudes are on display like fossil strata. Politics, that is, real arguments in politics; urgent debates about political economy, which are of drastic importance in Britain now; the fate of the world outside Britain; the culture of science and technology, the most powerful agents of change in our century; the really hard questions about the sustainability of our way of life – these debates are acknowledged, downloaded and filed outside the central memory.

These are large blind-spots, but beyond them again there is an ambiguous line where literature and culture start breaking down into mere speech. Most editors and publishers, me included, are terrified of the embarrassment that clutches at you from dealing with the unpolished records of peoples' lives, voices that are too rough, too raw or open. Of course there have to be standards of achievement, of expression and moral interest, but the relationship between the little tradition and the great tradition is not as clear cut as Alan Bloom liked to think. Urbane literary culture can be really rattled by voices from below.

The democratisation of culture as part of a democratic culture is not a programme of dilution or of nonsensical relativism. There are standards as I've said which it is empowering to master. Precisely because access to a voice is so bound up with wider political and social issues, it is possible to hope that a greater diversity of stories can and will be told, and make claims to be judged alongside, and to become as central as those stories we already know. This will not, in itself, improve the lot of those who are represented in them, but the inaudible are more easily brutalised. Black Americans and women of the developed world have hardly found utopia, but at least their increased access to a voice allows oppression to be described and contested.

The power to utter comes earlier than the power to edit, let alone to hire the editors. The situation of articulate minorities in

London publishing has already been described; and although the emergence of women in senior positions has definitely been a change for the better, with fresh attitudes and more democratic and open styles of management, and a real commitment to books by, for and about women, the larger picture is depressing. In the US, the informal racial frontiers meander through the bastions of culture. Years after the Civil Rights Acts, there are at most six black book editors in New York. The trade organ of US publishing recently quoted an editor at one of the leading houses as saying that "we" really underestimated the market for African-American writing and books of interest to blacks. The hidden history of exclusion and unconscious deselection that resonates through that admission is truly tragic.

Alertness and good intentions are never enough. To limit ourselves to Ireland and Britain, it is difficult to see any more democratic politics of reading, writing and publishing outside the framework of a quite fundamental democratic reform, which – especially in Britain – would also involve the adoption of the very idea of constitutional rights. If you do not have rights as a citizen of a constitutional state, you never speak in your own voice, except to vote passively twice a decade, and you are spoken to by the Crown-in-Parliament, which never has to hear your voice in order to do more or less what it likes: declare war, abolish local democracy, gag the papers, and surround the state with ring after ring of secrecy. Without a constitutional commitment to the right to know, equality of access to education, to local democracy, to the right of reply as well as to freedom of expression, and to some notion of a right to work, we may find ourselves deeper inside some very familiar and grim stories from our century, in which more and more of us are expected to remain silent.

Cathleen O'Neill

I AM THE other face of Kilbarrack, the other side of Barrytown as represented in *The Commmitments*. I am in the quiet, hard-working part of working-class culture that very seldom gets a positive representation in the media. I also come with loads of new terms. I know that I am a carrier of the killer strain; I am the voice from below and anathema to those above, hopefully and thankfully. I will let in the light or focus a spotlight on a culture that is too often misrepresented and misunderstood. I am a community arts worker. I want to illustrate how we use art as a vehicle for social and community change. In terms of censorship in the arts, I will be concentrating on how people in my community, in my social class, experience social control and censorship: education, the arts, language, value judgements, class discrimination, stereotyping and social exclusion.

I will place myself within that experience by relating the story of my adult education centre which is called KLEAR in Kilbarrack. In order to give you an insight into that experience and the reasons why our centre exists, I will read you a poem which shows the kinds of people who make up the community arts experience, come to adult education classes or arrive at our community education centre. I chose this poem because it focuses on censorship of the arts in terms of social exclusion. It was written in a cold classroom by a group of community writers. The woman who wrote the poem is one of a group of adults availing of second chance education, although seated at desks and on chairs designed for four year olds. The poem sets the theme of my presentation.

I am not what you see, this plain woman, not all of me
Life screens the essence of what I am
Through the days busy patchwork, I do what I can
To nourish a mind that screams to be freed
And I know I can do it, becomes my new creed.
My inner self just waiting the chance
To break loose from the bonds and adopt a new stance
To learn all I can and absorb every day
New thoughts, and ideas, the foundation lay
For the glorious day when I break through the mould,

Of class, gender and children, just watch me take hold.

The writer mentions class and gender as the controls that hold her. But she was in her middle years before she even found the time and the space to reflect on her experiences as an adult. The space she found was called KLEAR, an adult education centre pioneered and managed by five working-class women who wanted to avail of second chance education. KLEAR is now 12 years old. It is Ireland's oldest day-time adult education centre. It was and is a role model for other community groups. From the start, we offered childcare facilities at competitive rates. We paid our childcare workers the top rate. We designed our own classes, fund-raised and managed the centre, all in a voluntary capacity. We are still doing that although our numbers have grown to five hundred attending weekly. The adults who come here are availing of second chance and in many cases first chance education because they have been failed by the formal education system.

We have a thriving and absolutely dynamic literacy group. A hundred adults a week come to learn or to develop their reading and writing skills. We actually do not call it a literacy group because it would be referred to in the media as an *illiteracy* group. We offer community and action education. We also offer creative and community development education. It was to this area of KLEAR that the writer of the poem came.

KLEAR was Ireland's first writers' group, which founded many other writers' groups nationwide, both in Northern Ireland and in the South of Ireland. The first publication was called *From Wits End to Humble Beginnings*, and in many ways, we are still at our wits' end, although our beginnings are not so humble. Our first publication was made possible by the prison officers in Mountjoy Jail. Twelve years ago photocopying facilities were not as available as they are today. Our education centre had no funding, but one woman was married to a prison officer in Mountjoy who offered us the facilities at the prison to photocopy, lay up and paste. We have since published eight more books which are actually viable in a commercial sense; however, not many people know about them because censorship is a subtle thing.

The woman who wrote the poem is representative of the 500 adults who attend the centre, most of whom live on social welfare. She lives in an area where there is 52 per cent unemployment, and 63 per cent of the families in the area experience ongoing serious medical problems caused by poverty, unemployment and stress. She is representative of early school-leavers, the working-class, the unemployed – the 1.3 million poor that is quoted daily in the media. She is called a "unit of dependence". She came to KLEAR because we repair the damage caused by the formal education system. We provide access to education and creativity in an area that is fractured by unemployment and poverty. We counter society's narrow view of poverty which is the provision of the basics for physical survival. Ours is a broader view which takes into account people's other needs, which are social, emotional, political, cultural and artistic. But it is a long hard struggle. A struggle that is mirrored all over Ireland. What is going on at a micro level in Kilbarrack is going on nationwide. Our struggle is not aided by the state; in fact it is hindered by the state. Community funding is difficult to find. Instead, we find that we get the mushroom treatment, being kept in the dark more often than we get successful funding applications. Community funding from the Arts Council received two per cent of its total budget in 1991. I think that is an indication of their commitment to it. Our job is made difficult in terms of the fund-raising procedures required by the Department of Social Welfare. Our job is made difficult in terms of Ireland depending on voluntarism and the begging bowl, and by the nature of once-off projects which do not allow for development. Neither are we helped by the media, either the broadcasters or the print medium, who constantly stereotype us. I would like to give you a few examples of that now.

Often we get telephone calls into KLEAR from RTE and other community stations; they will want someone to talk about poverty or unemployment or being deserted, but they will not accept someone who is articulate. I have been turned down as a speaker on those issues because I am too articulate and not representative of the working class. I have that in writing. They want women who will expose themselves, who will tell their personal details because this makes for good broadcasting. They do not want women who are going to question the structures. They will say that it has already been covered but it has not been covered *by* us; it has been covered *for* us. I wrote my book *Telling It As It Is* (Combat Poverty, 1992) because I did not find myself represented in any of the plethora of research on poverty and unemployment that was done in the '80s. My book is a response to the fact that I never found myself represented there. I have never found my culture represented there. I never found any of the developments that I am involved in represented there. I just found middle-class views, outsider views of what was going on. Not insider views. So in KLEAR, and in my own personal life, we try all the time to address that.

Did you ever notice in advertising that working-class voices are always portrayed as germs, stains and smells? That is how we found ourselves being represented. In the print media we have not been treated very well either. It is significant to know that during Dublin Millennium 1991, the papers were daily full of complaints about the Millennium office staff and about what was being done for arts promotion. Nevertheless, it was the existence of the Millennium that allowed some of our groups to even explore areas of our creativity. We got seed funding to do things for which we would not otherwise have had access.

During the Millennium I designed the women's poster. The official version that went all round the world was a poster of eleven men. I think thirteen phallic symbols, including a pint of Guinness and a hurley, this was a thousand years of Dublin history and I tried to correct that by doing a women's poster, "The Spirit of Women". It was subsequently withdrawn from sale by the Millennium office because one of the managers objected to *sheelagh-na-gigs* around the border of the poster. He found it offensive. He also withdrew from sale the female half of a Viking couple because she had her breasts bared. Thus, censorship goes on at different levels.

There is a wonderful exhibition in IMMA at the Royal Hospital Kilmainham, called "The Unspoken Truths". It is an art exhibition produced by two community groups after eighteen months hard work. A leading journalist, in an article about the exhibition, chose to talk about the artist who came dressed in the best clothes of the poor. While the journalist went on to give a very good review of the exhibition, she still chose to highlight the fact that it was the "poor" who were actually the producers of the art. She did not see the political developments at all.

In KLEAR we are daily engaged in empowering people who have been made powerless by the state; not those who are personally powerless, but who have been made powerless by the state. We do that in a voluntary capacity. We have been doing it for 12 years, but despite our great success, we are this year facing our biggest threat to our survival – our school is being taken away from us. So even when you do get up off your knees, as the papers urge us constantly, pull ourselves up by our bootstraps, we still have no security.

David Collins

I WOULD LIKE to talk very briefly about the censorship of films in this country, and to recount certain experiences which I had over 15 years ago when I worked as the film officer of the Arts Council. Then I will discuss the contradictions which are involved in my job. I am a commercial animal; my job is to get commissions, get money from people to produce programmes that directors and film-makers want to make. Many of those stories come from the hinterland, but every day a person in my position makes either skilful or unskilful compromises. Finally, the big issue is, in some sense, that we are no longer telling our own stories – in particular, where current affairs coverage of Northern Ireland on television has been concerned over the last ten years plus.

About fifteen years ago or longer, I was the film officer of the Arts Council with a friend of mine, Kevin Rockett. We put together a special magazine on the subject of film censorship, for which I was paid by the Arts Council. One of the most extraordinary scenarios occurred at that stage. The film censor throughout most of the 1970s was a man called Dermot Breen, a very bright, intelligent, passionate man, who also happened to be the leading light at the Cork Film Festival. This was a job where the whole state was in effect relying on one man's moral integrity or personal taste. He described his role in a speech to the Cork Rotary Club.

I interpret a film through what I would like my children – and they range from ten to 19 – to see. The kind of book I might like to read I won't leave lying around at home for my son to read. I certainly wouldn't put a picture on the wall that I thought might give my children wrong ideas about life. We have certain moral standards that we must uphold. I'm appointed by the minister and given a certain job to do. There are certain (I won't say restrictions) guidelines laid down. I try to follow these guidelines as best I can and be as flexible as I can. But there are limitations.

When we produced this magazine in the Arts Council, we got into a certain amount of hot water. It was worse when the Arts Council decided to set up its own exhibition structure, which in turn set up an organisation called The Irish Film Theatre. That was my first encounter with the conflicts that start to arise between commercial considerations and one's desire to let everybody have their say.

The Irish Film Theatre was a subsidiary of the Arts Council and was run on a commercial basis, because there were no funds with the Arts Council to subsidise the IFT. It had to break even. Also, the Arts Council did not have the money to pay the costs of censoring films, which are still very high. These costs are a barrier on any structure unless it operates on a membership basis, with membership in name only. The cost of censoring *E.T.* is the same as the cost of censoring an art house film that might play for one night in front of a commercial audience in town. When the Irish Film Theatre was established, we had huge hits like films like *Last Tango in Paris,* but we had the "dirty mac" brigade. The IFT was a commercial success at that time, but I used to get letters addressed to "The Irish Sex Theatre". I only say this because I think most of these problems have gone away, but the core issue remains: that the state, for whatever reasons, has decided that there will be a person who is a film censor. This is interesting because it does not exist in any visible way in any of the other art forms. It may be implied, but it certainly does not exist in any formal or structured way. Moreover, the censors operated the ultimate censorship on themselves, because when the Arts Council produced the magazine they did not tell their own stories. The censor at the time, Mr Frank Hall, declined to participate in it.

Three of the censors were actually medical doctors, which gives me an opportunity for a metaphor. It is that film censorship is really akin to an act of surgery – cutting out the offending tissue. You cut out tissue in a body that might be otherwise healthy and, unlike other forms of censorship, film censorship is much more in the style of re-writing sentences in a book. One could argue that the better or the more classic the censorship, the more seamless the end result. And even still, there are numerous films on video and in the cinemas which are censored. There are numerous films which are seen on television in versions completely different from those seen on the screen, and that is part of the process. But it is the seamlessness of it, the fact that it is very difficult to distinguish. The major issue is why there should be a film censor. Why should there be a person? Why in the early 1990s do we still invest one person with this moral authority? Is that a good way of doing it?

Two current stories in which I am involved as a television pro-

ducer reflect on points that have been raised. We have a contract
with RTE, the state broadcaster, to produce a programme about
the deaf community in Ireland, which is researched and presented
by people who are deaf. We are on record as saying that we would
like as soon as possible for our independent production company
structure to fall away so that the programme can actually be produced by deaf people. The whole programme should be their programme. This, however, has been not accepted by the broadcaster.
I find that odd. We are currently in production on a documentary
on ILGO, the Irish Lesbian and Gay Organisation, in New York,
who have been prevented in the last two years from marching as
gays and lesbians in the St Patrick's Day parade. We began that
story from our own resources. The only support we received was
from Virgin Airways, not Aer Lingus, because I felt sponsorship
was an important consideration. ILGO have now won their court
case. The documentary [broadcast on RTE on 23 March 1993] reflects ILGO's victory over the Ancient Order of Hibernians
(AOH). We have become a mediator of their story, through a contract which we have with the broadcaster. This is not ILGO telling
their own story to the Irish public. This is our company having received a commission to tell a story about a victory in New York.

These are complex editorial problems which have to be resolved
on a day to day basis, but they are more than skirmishes for the
people involved. They are more than skirmishes for the deaf community, who do not have direct access to making their programmes. It is more than a skirmish for ILGO. They would be
considered a special interest group, yet why should they not have
the right to tell their side of the story on public television?
However, the big issue, the most insidious issue, is the one that
concerns me as a viewer more than as a producer. That is the coverage of Northern Ireland over the last ten years.

It is really difficult to point a finger, but it does strike me that
programmes like *Shooting to Kill*, *Death on the Rock* and programmes on the Guildford Four and the Birmingham Six – high
budget, detailed programmes with high production values at-
tracting huge audiences – have been exclusively made by well-
meaning and well-motivated people almost within the ITV system
exclusively. The argument has often been made that we do not
have the resources to make these programmes within Ireland. I accept that the economics of broadcasting here are extremely tight.

But it does strike me that it is convenient; it was convenient that the Beef Tribunal was based upon a Granada television programme. We conveniently applaud the courage of British television producers and researchers as they stand on the steps of a court having either won or lost a court case over a programme about our country and our dilemma that they have told.

POLITICAL CENSORSHIP

Mary Holland

ONE THREAD FOR this part of the conference is contained in Salman Rushdie's point that once decent reasons are found for a little bit of censorship, quickly other freedoms and freedom of access to information disappear. How easy it is to find reasons for increased censorship. We live in a state where there are constantly reasons given as to why information should be denied for what many people consider are reasonable reasons. The second thread was referred to by Carl Bernstein when he talked about the standard of journalism. The most important weapon that journalists have is the quality of their work, and that quality is necessary to get the best available version of the truth. By "available" Bernstein meant that it is the duty of journalists, as trade unionists, as citizens, to keep pushing out the boundaries to get to the truth. Anyone who has been censored or has had pressure put on them knows how easy it is to slip into self-censorship. Over time, that becomes more of a threat than the ban, the court case or the injunction; it is difficult to resist. Yet, if journalists are to give readers, viewers and the public the best available version of the truth, it is essential.

This session is called political censorship. While all censorship is political, there are overt forms of censorship which are imposed either by the state itself or through its instruments – the courts, the legal system and so on – such as the broadcasting bans in both parts of Ireland. Women suffer from censorship – the ban on abortion information – imposed by this state, but hopefully now to be lifted. The organised resistance to Section 31 may not have appeared much, but it has been heroic and consistent compared with the resistance by journalists and broadcasting media organisations to the ban on abortion information. Magazines and newspapers, British and Irish, have connived at the censorship and volunteered to censor their own papers on the question of abortion information. To my knowledge there has been no organised resistance to this at all by the broadcasting organisations. It is an issue which women have to take on, but why has it never become an issue with journalists or magazines or the unions within magazines or the unions within the newspapers?

Alex White

IN 1991 THE European Commission for Human Rights in Strasbourg rejected the case against Section 31 brought by the two broadcast unions in this country, the NUJ and SIPTU. Section 31 is part of a complex of constraints and restrictions, a form of censorship, which operates in this country – some of which are highly visible and many invisible. Without any doubt, Section 31 is the most visible and damaging form of political censorship. The issue of Section 31 must be raised publicly, not in an isolated way as in the past, but must form part of a wider campaign for freedom of expression and democracy and against censorship and secrecy in Ireland.

Section 31 is part of the 1960 Broadcasting Act which regulates RTE, to which there was an amendment in 1976. Under the terms of that act, the Minister for Communications can order the RTE Authority, and now the independent sector, to refrain from broadcasting

any matter or any matter of a particular class which he or she believes would be likely to promote or incite to crime or would tend to undermine the authority of the state.

Ministerial orders, with little variation, have been renewed annually in mid-January for the last 17 years, and have restricted broadcasters from carrying particular interviews. The current order was introduced in the mid-1970s:

that the broadcasters are instructed to refrain from broadcasting an interview or a report of an interview with a spokesman or with spokesmen for any one or more of the following organisations, namely, the organisation styling itself the Irish Republican Army also the IRA and Óglaigh na hÉireann, Sinn Féin, Republican Sinn Féin, the UDA, the INLA, and finally any organisation which in Northern Ireland is a proscribed organisation for the purposes of Section 21 of the Act of the British Parliament entitled the Northern Ireland Emergency Provisions Act 1978.

Effectively, the order automatically includes any organisation covered under the Emergency Provisions Act in Northern Ireland. Two additional provisions in relation to party political broadcasts are also in operation.

The order is made for a maximum of one year. It has been re-newed annually for the past 17 years without any debate, discus-sion, objection or insistence that the government put forward its rationale to the Oireachtas. In this context, it is not surprising that a former Taoiseach, Garret FitzGerald, admitted that the issue of freedom of information had never struck him as being important, nor had he had much opportunity to think about it, although he would be prepared to listen to a debate about it.

I want to refer in some detail to the less visible effects of the order issued under Section 31: reports that never appear on radio or television, and programmes that are never made. Examples are difficult to recount because the effect of Section 31 is to prevent journalists and programme-makers doing their job: to report the facts; to tell the full story, not half the story; to produce for the audience the best obtainable version of the truth; and to provide a credible medium for the views and the experience of everyone in the community, not just those who are regarded as politically ac-ceptable or politically respectable by those in power. Salman Rushdie made this point eloquently when he said freedom of speech is very easy in relation to the views you like. The real test, the true test, is whether we allow views on the airwaves and in public of those we do not like – especially the views we find repre-hensible or loathsome. That is the test that we fail in relation to Section 31. I cannot see that there is any doubt about it.

I am not assuming, by the way, that everybody believes that the views of the banned organisations are loathsome. Yet, in its place, radio and television should record a plurality of views, of experi-ences, of information. Coverage of the political situation in the North, and of the national question, is without any question deeply affected and distorted by Section 31. A comprehensive pro-gramme on the North, one which is balanced and informative, cannot be made by RTE. There are whole areas of everyday life, especially in Northern Ireland, which are more or less completely excluded from any coverage, presence or involvement on radio and television.

A further issue concerns RTE's interpretation of Section 31, which is currently before the Supreme Court. RTE has argued that any *member* of a proscribed organisation, which might in fact be legally registered as a political party in this state, is automatically banned from the airways irrespective of the subject matter. This Supreme Court case involves RTE's refusal to interview Larry O'Toole, a spokesman for workers on strike at the Gateaux factory in Dublin during 1990, because he was a *member* of Sinn Féin, a proscribed organisation. The current case essentially claims that RTE's interpretation of the ministerial order is too broad and incorrect in law. The results of the judgement will have huge implications for the way in which the order is operated.*

There have been some bizarre examples under this particular interpretation of Section 31, not least of which was the famous Marcus Free case, the famous mushroom case. During an RTE radio phone-in programme, Marcus Free was about to discuss the suitability of mushrooms for wine production when he was told that as a member of Sinn Féin there could be no interview. Whatever else Sinn Féin does, it does not have a particular involvement or expertise in wine making; although his party membership was completely immaterial to the subject, he was excluded from the programme. In another example, the main eyewitness to a serious fire in Bundoran some years ago was discovered to be a member of Sinn Féin just before air-time, and could not be interviewed. Eileen Flynn could not be interviewed about her unfair dismissal case before the Employment Appeals Tribunal for similar reasons. In case after case, people have been excluded from interview on the grounds of Sinn Féin membership, even when they are involved in debates on issues which have nothing to do with the political situation. Whatever about the existence of the order, effectively its implementation has become too restrictive.

Elections, general elections, local elections, elections to the European parliament: these are rightly regarded by many people as important occasions in the democratic process. The true effect of Section 31, and the contradictions inherent in it, are illustrated most harshly during election time and during the results coverage afterwards. Since the order began, RTE journalists have been prevented from interviewing candidates, successful or otherwise, in any election who are members of proscribed organisations. This is

---

*Conor Cruise O'Brien, who as minister between 1973-1977 was an architect of the present order and has remained a firm supporter of it, last year criticised RTE's interpretation.

the case, despite the fact that these organisations and political parties, although named in the ministerial order, are not illegal. In contrast, the ban in Britain is more liberal because it sets aside broadcasting restrictions at election times. Instead, RTE journalists must interview defeated candidates where a banned candidate has won. The ban prohibits both a direct interview, and a report and discussion of an interview which a broadcast presenter had conducted with a member of a listed organisation. The latter would be regarded as a report of an interview. Thus, in the 1989 general election, for example, when Christy Burke came close to taking a seat in Dublin Central, there could not be an interview or a report of an interview with him. Gerry Adams could not be interviewed when he lost his West Belfast seat in 1992, but neither could Sinn Féin candidates be included in any pre-election reports or constituency profiles.

Section 31 has an even wider effect in practice. In an atmosphere affected by the continued use of Section 31, in places like RTE, there has been an insidious and damaging tendency for many journalists and programme-makers to avoid areas of investigation or debate which might conceivably run into problems associated with Section 31. Journalists have opted not to attend a press conference about a local environment issue when it became known that Sinn Féin members were actively involved, and that there would be little likelihood of being able to broadcast interviews with these same local activists. Journalists have decided that they do not want the hassle of going to a press conference, and asking people if they are members of Sinn Féin, although they may suspect or have been told that they are; after all, there are two or three other good stories knocking around in the newsroom. This is the day to day reality for journalists and editors. There is usually another story.

This is the same situation, by extension, that led to British television stations exposing the Birmingham and Guildford scandals. It was not RTE. We are way behind with these stories. It's an undeniable fact that RTE's coverage of Northern Ireland is not very good. Although RTE has offices in Belfast, there are many journalists and producers who would never even consider doing a programme in the North, many who have never travelled North. The unfortunate fact is that after 17 years, few people will take risks, particularly where there is very little encouragement from anybody to push out the barriers of its operation. Many in RTE remember

Jenny McGeever, who was dismissed from RTE about four years ago for allegedly breaching Section 31 in a report about the funerals following the killing of three alleged IRA people in Gibraltar.

A whole generation of journalists have come into RTE since the 1970s and have never worked in broadcasting without the restrictions under Section 31. Section 31 has become institutionalised, normalised, part of the culture. Because it is accepted, it is difficult to get the issue raised or challenged, or to push out the boundaries. James Downey put the issue in *Business and Finance*:

If an editor or producer in RTE appears to deviate in the smallest way from the restrictions, or calls attention to their ill effects on his work, that proves his unsoundness. If on the other hand, he applies them with the greatest stringency, that proves he is trying to bring them into disrepute. Damned if you do; damned if you don't.

This issue of soundness is an interesting concept, and one that raises its ugly head from time to time in RTE, although not so much in recent times. During 1987-88, a serious and potentially ugly episode rocked RTE around the time of the Enniskillen atrocity, although it continued to reverberate for a couple of years after that. Some in RTE who supported Section 31 openly accused others who opposed it of being dodgy on terrorism, the IRA, or political violence. In mine and other cases, various posters and leaflets were distributed, put on notice-boards and shoved under office doors around the management floor, alleging that people were silent supporters of Provisional Sinn Féin, otherwise termed "hush puppies". While these actions could be dismissed as being the eccentric ramblings of a particular individual, it did not encourage others in RTE that the time was right to oppose Section 31. Rather, it contributed to a particular atmosphere.

I am very conscious of what Carl Bernstein said about the responsibility on journalists and programme-makers. I do not believe that journalists have been strong enough on this issue. Throughout the late 1970s and early 1980s, virtually nothing happened on the issue except for a one-day strike, pickets on Dáil Éireann, and meetings with politicians. The single biggest action was the enormous work that went into gathering a legal challenge to Section 31. Seventeen RTE journalists and producers took the Irish government to the European Commission on Human Rights, challenging Section 31 under a number of different provisions of the European Convention on Human Rights. We had been very confident on the basis of the work put into that case that it would win, but the case was lost. The Commission decided, after an oral hearing and written evidence, that the restrictions contained in Section 31 were justified in the context of the violent threat to the state represented by organisations such as the IRA, and by extension, Sinn Féin. The Commission's rationale reflected the Irish government's case, which is particularly disturbing.

The government claimed it was trying to prevent the airwaves from being used or manipulated by terrorists, advocating terrorism or promoting or inciting violence. But there is another section of the 1960 Broadcasting Act, Section 18, which excludes that type of material from the airwaves. The real effect and intention of Section 31 is to exclude not just the views or the statements of members of these listed organisations, but to keep the individuals themselves off the airwaves. It is to deny them respectability or legitimacy, which the government believes automatically flows from an appearance on radio or television. The government does not conceal this intent; to allow a spokesman from Sinn Féin to appear on television and be interviewed would suggest that the organisation represented by him is no different from any other political party which upholds the constitution and the democratic nature of the state. The appearance by this person, whoever he or she might be, might directly incite persons to crime.

This is a very depressing and outdated theory of radio and television. During the 1920s Walter Lippman coined a phrase to describe the widespread view that information communicated through the media had a direct and profound influence on a passive audience, who simply gulped it down without any discernment. He called it the "magic bullet" theory of communication. That was in the 1920s, but in the 1990s the European Commission on Human Rights could say the following:

In contemporary society, radio and television are medias with considerable powers of influence. Their impact is more immediate than that of the print media and the possibilities of the broadcaster to correct, qualify, interpret or comment on any statement made on radio or television or limit – in comparison with those available to journalists in the press – live statements could also involve a special risk of coded messages being conveyed, a risk which even conscientious journalists cannot control within the exercise of their professional judgement.

This is a remarkably depressing and dated view of the media and its impact.

The audience does not consist of passive dupes, but rather active, selective and discerning people in their use of the media. The idea that people can simply be triggered like a gun if somebody says something on television, that they will shoot the first British soldier or policeman they see, beggars belief as a way of understanding the media. But this is the view of the Irish government, and is the only effort by the government to rationalise Section 31 of which I am aware. Although the case was lost, the exercise of setting down on paper the effects of Section 31 was very valuable. Seventeen affidavits described, in case after case, how Section 31 operates in everyday life. The book of affidavits can still be valuably used.

In conclusion, at no stage was it argued in Strasbourg by the applicants that the broadcast media either should or could be used as a platform for promoting terrorism. Instead, it was argued that the restrictions in Section 31 go way beyond the objective of preventing the media being used for incitement. Rather, it prevented the media doing its job: reporting facts and facilitating informed public debate. Michael D. Higgins, now Minister for Arts, Culture and the Gaeltacht, supported the public statement that led to the setting up of this conference. The minimum requirement now is for a review and debate on Section 31. Politicians will only respond to pressure to abolish this draconian piece of legislation and open the airwaves to all points of view.

Jake Ecclestone

I WOULD LIKE to begin with a few words, by way of a prologue. First, I cannot help feeling that censorship stalks this island like a ghost. The man most censored is not here to speak about what it's like and we should think about that. Second, journalism is the first rough draft of history. That's an imaginative description, but quite true. The problem is that if you live in a censored society, then the very first rough draft of history is distorted and false. If our children grow up in a society which has got a false view of its own history, then we are in deep trouble. I come from a society greatly responsible for some of this censorship.

One of my jobs for the NUJ is to help our members in matters of press and broadcasting freedom, and I want to talk about some of the various forms of censorship which exist in Britain. Some of you will have experienced this in your own way; all of them exist in Northern Ireland.

Since all British governments have refused to incorporate the European Convention on Human Rights into British law, I have no absolute right to freedom of speech. Similarly, as they have refused to introduce freedom of information legislation, I have no right to know what is being done in my name. Public life in Britain is therefore extremely fertile ground for secrecy, and it is a very easy step from secrecy to censorship. Indeed, arguably, they are two sides of the same coin.

Censorship in Britain comes in an extraordinary variety of forms. First, there is an obsession in Britain for secrecy, beginning with the basic military form pioneered during the Crimean War and improved in the Boer War, and brought to a pitch ten years ago during the Falkland Islands War. At that time, the government had the capacity to put all journalists on board their ships so that all reports had to go through government communications channels. That is certainly the best form of war censorship. You will recall that the Americans picked up many British ideas during the Gulf War two years ago, to such an extent that I bought *The Irish Times* in London because I could not trust British newspapers.

Second, there is censorship by statute, laws like the Official Secrets Act 1911, which went through parliament in approximately 45 minutes and remained in force until three years ago when ministers claimed that it was reformed and liberalised. But that was not the case. The new Official Secrets Act in Britain hangs like a dead weight over British public servants. The Prevention of Terrorism Act – legislation passed in great haste is always bad law – went through parliament in 24 hours in 1974, and although it is useless for preventing terrorism, it has oppressive side-effects. A few years ago, for example, a British television company was fined £70,000 for refusing to disclose the identity of informants on a programme alleging collusion between government officials and Protestant gunmen in Northern Ireland. Section 28 of the Local Government Act 1987, forbids local authorities to allow any information to be published or provided by local authorities regarding homosexuality.

Third, there is judge-made censorship; Irish judges are just as adept at inventing new laws. The *Spycatcher* affair, 1986-89, was a good example. The Thatcher government and senior civil servants lied in courtrooms all over the world in a desperate and, happily, unavailing attempt to prevent publication of the book. British judges went absolutely to the limit to construct new laws about confidentiality and the duties of former government servants, including proposing a novel use of injunctions. Having got injunctions against two newspapers, the government then sought to persuade judges, a couple of years later, that the original injunctions applied to all newspapers in Britain, which, of course, is an extremely dangerous extension of the use of injunctions. Happily, during 1992, that was set aside at the House of Lords.

Fourth, there is self-censorship. We all self-censor. Britain has brought censorship to an art form through the D-Notice Committee. This is a particularly odious form of self-censorship by the people who edit newspapers and run our television system, because only the very senior, carefully hand-picked people from the media serve on D-notice committees. "D" stands for Defence and Broadcasting Committee. The committee was established in 1912 to buttress the Official Secrets Act; British newspaper editors and more recently broadcasting executives sit solemnly alongside superannuated rear admirals and senior civil servants from the Ministry of Defence deciding what should not be published in the public interest or rather in the state's interest. Books, newspapers, etc. go to the D-Notice Committee. Although it does not have any legal backing, it has had quite a chilling effect on British journalism.

Two years ago, for example, at a seminar organised by the International Press Institute, various senior newspaper people and broadcasters defended the system, including John Birt, the new Director General of the BBC. He described it as "a valuable forum" and "an effective system". What is particularly dreadful about the D-notice system is that representatives and powerful figures within the media are integrated with government officials who quite deliberately and cynically seek to restrain information. The absurdity about the D-notice system is that it operates with no force of law. The notices themselves contain rather antiquated and turgid prose about state security. Paragraph 1 of D-notice 6 seeks to protect Britain; it says:

> The broad functions of the security and intelligence services are widely known in that they are responsible for countering the threat to the realm arising from espionage to subversion and sabotage and for providing her Majesty's government with secret intelligence concerning foreign powers. These services must work, as far as possible, in conditions of secrecy. The publication of detailed information about any activities or methods or the disclosure of identities is likely to prejudice both present and past operations and also to make more difficult the day to day work of persons involved.

Although 99 per cent plus of British journalists have never seen these notices, they act as a terrible anchor on what can or can not be reported.

A funny story about D-notice activities concerns book publishing. Some years ago there was an attempt to publish a book about breaking the German Enigma code machine at Bletchley, during the Second World War, after which British Intelligence was able to read German codes. Apparently the reason the D-notice Committee and the security services were anxious to avoid publishing how the British cracked the Enigma machine was quite simple. When the war finished, Britain sold a number of these machines to unsuspecting third world countries. Why do you think the British government did not want these countries knowing that the code had been cracked?

Fifth, government ministers are given power under the various acts to issue ministerial orders, similar to Section 31. (It is a terrible indictment of British society that the NUJ is the only body that has challenged the government.) There is also the power of ministers to issue what they falsely claim to be public interest immunity certificates. A few weeks ago, Michael Heseltine issued such a certificate to prevent information being presented to a court which was then trying two British business men for supplying arms to Iraq. He failed in this attempt, but if he had succeeded it is possible these men would have gone to jail, although they were working for British military intelligence while selling arms to Iraq. Of course, Michael Heseltine knew that; therefore one must assume that the government was willing to see two innocent men (if you can say that about arms dealers) being sent to prison when they had actually been working for the British state.

Sixth, a particularly chilling type of censorship is the use of violence. In spite of the appalling catalogue of sectarian murders in Northern Ireland over the last two decades, there have mercifully been relatively few acts of violence against journalists. However, on 1 October 1992, a man went into the office of the *Sunday World*, put a gun to the head of a young female secretary, and left a bomb. The bomb did not go off, but the intent was to kill all the journalists in that office. In this context of physical threats to journalists, during 1992 the INLA (Irish National Liberation Army) issued threats to journalists working on the *Irish News*, the *Sunday News* and the *Sunday World*. The NUJ has protested against what these sectarian groups are doing, standing up and speaking out for our members, and I would like to pay tribute to Jim Campbell of the *Sunday World*. Nine years ago, gunmen put two bullets into his chest; he almost died, but came back to work and was still working in his office when a bomb was planted there last October. In spite of these appalling incidents, he has not been frightened off. Campbell is a very brave man and I hope readers of his newspaper appreciate the extraordinary lengths to which he goes to secure the truth for them.

Seven, there are in Britain the Thirty Year Rule, the Seventy-five Year Rule and the never rule. The never rule is the one that you never see. Every year, newspapers rush to the public records office to read released government papers, but there is a certain cynicism about this exercise, because despite the Thirty Year Rule, all the documents have been meticulously weeded by the civil servants whose job it is ensure that nobody is embarrassed.

Eight, Privy Council laws reinforce the Official Secrets Act to ensure that government ministers do not step out of line and talk too much about what they did when in office.

And finally, nine, there is fear. Fear permeates society. Once you get into the position where you could lose your job, be held up to ridicule, held up to attack by certain newspapers, fear is a far more effective method of censoring than ministerial certificates because it works silently, it works in the nooks and crannies of society. No one or very few will ever admit to fear which leads them to censor themselves. A quote from a leading article in the *Times* – not the degraded version presently run by Rupert Murdoch, but an earlier and altogether more honourable newspaper – was one of the best enunciations of the duties of the press:

> The first duty of the press is to obtain the earliest and most correct intelligences of the event in time, and, instantly, by disclosing, to make them the common property of the nation. A statesman collects his information secretly, and by secret means... The press lives by disclosure. The duty of the one is to speak, the other to be silent.

I think it is all our duty to speak.

Bill Rolston

THE TROUBLES IN Northern Ireland are at the core of censorship policy in these islands. Philip Schlesinger, a sociologist who researched the BBC and wrote a definitive book on media coverage of Northern Ireland in 1978, said

Ministerial intervention has been elusive and there was nothing in the BBC's approach to editorial control which approximated to the popular image regarding classic totalitarian censorship with its directives and specially planted supervisory personnel.

While Schlesinger is not suggesting this, there is a danger of concluding from this that the term "censorship" only applies to the classic totalitarian form. I am arguing that there are more subtle and often more efficient ways of censorship in democratic societies and the case of broadcasting in these islands shows that very clearly. These laws have been mentioned often. It seems to me that the states in Ireland and Britain have enough legal instruments at their disposal to ensure that something approximating classic totalitarian censorship of broadcasting could actually exist. If we start with Britain in Northern Ireland, there is direct legal regulation of broadcasting through the BBC licensing agreement and the Broadcasting Act of 1981. There is also legislation not directly designed to control broadcasting but which can affect broadcasting. For example, the Official Secrets Act 1911; Section 2 created over 2,000 offences, many of which can be applied to journalists and broadcasters. Section 1 allows for prosecution for possession of material prejudicial to the security of the state. The Northern Ireland Criminal Law Act 1967 makes it an offence for anyone, including a journalist or broadcaster, to refuse to give information to the police which the latter may wish to know. The British Contempt of Court Act 1981 prohibits the disclosure of any information or speculation which might be prejudicial to a current or pending court case. The Police and Criminal Evidence Act 1984, in Britain, says that the police can seize documents. Journalistic material is specifically excluded from that power; however, photographs are not and, in particular, photographs of any public event – for example, a march or a demonstration.

In Britain and Northern Ireland there is emergency legislation which can be used against broadcasters and journalists. The two most obvious acts are the Emergency Provisions Act 1978, which prohibits collecting, recording, publishing or attempting to elicit information, including photographs concerning the army, police, judges, court officials or prison officers which could be of use to terrorists. The Prevention of Terrorism Act 1989 says that citizens have a duty to tell the police anything which might prevent an act of terrorism or might help the police apprehend a terrorist.

In the Republic of Ireland, the Broadcasting Act 1960 and amended in 1976, seeks to control broadcasters. The Wireless and Telegraphy Act and the Radio and Television Act extend these controls to the commercial sector. Beyond direct laws for broadcasters there are other laws which are usable. The Offences Against the State Act 1939 and the Defamation Act 1961, can be used against broadcasters and journalists. The Official Secrets Act 1963 was modelled on the 1911 British Act, the only difference being now that the British, realising how bad it was, updated and amended theirs in 1989. There is no contempt of court act but there is the force of Common Law, and search and seizure provisions under a number of acts such as the Offences Against the State Act.

These laws are not mere sabre rattling on the part of the states in Britain and Ireland. These laws can be and are used, some examples of which have been referred to by others. In 1971, a journalist from Britain was jailed for four days in Northern Ireland under contempt of court legislation for refusing to identify someone he had interviewed as being the person before the court. The Official Secrets Act in Britain has been used against civil servants, but also against journalists such as Duncan Campbell and others in 1979 who were, interestingly, charged not just under Section 2 – possession of official information – but under Section 1 – treason. In fact, the Section 1 case collapsed, and under Section 2 they received very light sentences. But that is not the point.

Emergency legislation has been used in Northern Ireland to detain broadcasters and journalists and, in particular, photographers. A fairly recent example was in 1988: a German freelance photographer, Nick Voldo, was arrested under the Prevention of Terrorism Act after taking photographs of the police in action. He was charged with possession of arms, and let out on bail on condition that he would leave the country. The case was later dropped.

Use of the Prevention of Terrorism Act was threatened in an attempt to acquire film from broadcasting organisations regarding the Carrickmore IRA road block in 1979, and the killing of the two British army corporals in Andersonstown in 1988. It was successfully used to bring Channel 4 to court in 1992 over a *Dispatches* programme alleging loyalist and police collusion. A researcher for that programme, Ben Hamilton, was later arrested for perjury on the basis of an affidavit he made in that case. And finally, under the Criminal Evidence Act, it is now commonplace for police to ask for and get photographs and footage from photographers after every demonstration or march. In the Republic, Section 31 has allowed for the dismissal of the entire RTE Authority in 1972. In 1972 Kevin O'Kelly was sentenced to three months in prison under almost identical circumstances as Bernard Falk had been in Northern Ireland – refusing to identify someone he had interviewed. It also enabled the sacking of Jenny McGeever in 1988. The Offences Against the State Act was used in 1988 to impose a five-year prison sentence on Don O'Leary for possession of a republican poster, sold openly.

There is a remarkable range of repressive legislation in Northern Ireland and Britain, and a wide and unspecific set of powers for one particular law in the South. But to play devil's advocate for a second, Section 31 and the British broadcasting ban notwithstanding, the amount of direct control of broadcasters through such repressive legislation is, on a world scale, relatively light. The laws are not designed for control of broadcasters and are rarely used to do so. When they have been used, as in the case of the Official Secrets Act in Britain, they have been remarkably ineffectual. As for legislation directed specifically at controlling broadcasters, only one broadcaster in the North and one in the South have been jailed in the entire two decades of coverage of the Northern troubles. Only two broadcasters in the South have been sacked and none in the North. Broadcasting law does not operate through the daily intervention of state censors, the daily involvement of state imposed officials in decision-making within the broadcasting organisations, or the continuous daily axing of programmes after they have been made.

This is not the stuff of classic totalitarian censorship, yet this is not the end of the story. The laws work at a number of levels to control broadcasting. First, they are a constant backdrop, influencing consciously or otherwise decision-making and distorting professional practice. Their use is frequently threatened in no uncertain terms. For example, in a series of battles between Thatcher and broadcasters in the 1980s, the use of the Prevention of Terrorism Act was frequently threatened against broadcasters and the act was finally used in the case of Channel 4.

Second, even though the actual use of these laws has been relatively infrequent, there have been some spectacular outcomes. There are frequently differences between broadcasters and governments in any country, but as Betty Purcell has said in relation to RTE:

> In the atmosphere of daily censorship, managers learn that most conflicts blow over. Only on the sensitive subject of Northern Ireland have heads rolled and these were the most important heads in the organisation. Those of the RTE Authority itself.

Such cases act as exemplars and become part of the folk memory in broadcasting organisations. It only takes one such case every decade or so to remind everybody to be cautious.

Third, the main control of broadcasters now is through directives which are relatively imprecise, in both their content and their threatened sanctions. Section 31 and the British broadcasting ban do not operate by involving the state directly in the day to day running of these organisations. Rather they issue a blanket warning and leave both the implementation and the policing to the organisations themselves. A prime example here is the sacking of the RTE Authority in 1972. It was issued with a directive which was imprecise; it asked for further clarification, did not get it, and then when a report of an interview with Seán MacStiofan was carried, it was sacked. In effect, the message of the state was, we will not tell you what the limits are, but we will let you know forcibly enough if and when you transgress them. Article 19, the anti-censorship organisation, refers to this as a form of prior restraint censorship: it threatens action if a ban is broken rather than responding to specific broadcasts. That is an incredibly powerful control mechanism. It works by imposing caution on the broadcasting organisations themselves. It must be remembered that there was already a high level of caution within the organisations before such directives were issued in Ireland or Britain. In a very general sense, this caution is part of the trade-off which professional journalism and broadcasting has had to make historically with the state. Its independence from the state is predicated on the promise of "responsible behaviour".

Additionally, caution is needed when covering the issue of violence and, particularly, violence against a state which is seen to be democratic. Caution can be relaxed a bit if consensual opinion has it that the state concerned is not democratic and even more if it is far away. Thus, Sandy Gall can rough it with the Mujahadeen in Afghanistan, but what if it is an IRA active service unit in South Armagh?

In RTE the caution was formalised and institutionalised under Section 31. In fact, ritual references to the existence of Section 31 have allowed top management in RTE to take a very flexible line. Government directives ban interviews or reports of interviews with spokespersons of a number of organisations including Sinn Féin. But RTE has gone far beyond the spirit of the law to ban not just spokespersons but members. In addition, it has also been very quick to apply the ban to people under Section 18 of the Broadcasting Act who are not Sinn Féin members: Martin Galvin of NORAID and Nell McCafferty. Furthermore, RTE has acted ruthlessly and almost without fail against those who have broken the rules, even inadvertently or technically. The guidelines of RTE are very threatening in this respect:

> The strictest care must be taken in these matters and action will be called for where individuals are seen to have disregarded the guidelines or to have been careless in observing them.

As Jenny McGeever found out in 1988, that was no idle threat.

How can tough management justify this unprecedented interference with the freedom of the media? There is a paradox here. It is they who interpret the law inflexibly. They who police the restrictions on a daily basis. They who appeal court cases which might lead to liberalisation, thus reinforcing inflexibility. They who sack the offenders, and yet they, as part of the professional ideology of broadcasters, are the ones to whom censorship is anathema. To me this is a paradox; to Wesley Boyd, Head of News, it is not. As he told the International Federation of Journalists:

> We have been told we could interpret the law more liberally. We find that by sticking to the letter we can show how stupid it is.

The end result is that there is very little scope for challenge or subversion within RTE. I refer again to Betty Purcell:

> The question automatically asked is not what or who is in Sinn

Féin but who is definitely not in Sinn Féin.

To challenge this ritual is to run the risk of being labelled a "Provo-lover". The bottom line is that when this happens it is not just the grand ideals of democracy, freedom of the media or freedom of expression which are at stake, it is much more the down to earth reality of pay and promotion.

The case is somewhat different with the BBC, ITV and Channel 4. The broadcasting ban has been formalised relatively recently but it has served to emphasise that it works by emphasising a caution which is already built into the British broadcasting system over two decades. In the initial flurry of enthusiasm over civil rights, British broadcasters quickly found that covering Northern Ireland led to confrontations with the Right, both inside and outside government. After a number of run-ins, most notably and most spectacularly over a programme called "A Question of Ulster", in late 1971, an institutionalised caution, called a reference-up system, was introduced into the BBC and ITV. All items on Northern Ireland were to be referred to high levels of management, sometimes even to Director Generals or the Independent Broadcasting Authority itself. Liz Curtis described this system:

> On virtually every other topic, programme editors, producers, and journalists are trusted to make appropriate decisions about what subjects to select and how to present them. They are expected to refer to their superiors for guidance only in cases of real doubt or difficulty. On Ireland, however, no one was to be trusted.

Roger Bolton, as a nuance to Curtis's general conclusion, claimed that such a massive amount of output meant delegation was inevitable, but referenced up only when necessary. This system did allow senior management a way out. If there was no trouble, reference up worked perfectly. If there was, they had not been sufficiently put in the picture and assistants' heads must roll.

This control, this reference-up system, covers a whole set of guidelines. BBC guidelines on the use of language are among my favourite:

> We call it the army and its personnel soldiers, not the British army or British soldiers when they are in Northern Ireland. The Irish Republican Army: it is never acceptable to call them that, it is acceptable to call them the Provisionals but never the Provos. Don't give pet names to terrorists... don't speak of IRA volun-

teers, we don't know why they joined.

Despite these guidelines, people like Roger Bolton, Paul Hamann and others ran into trouble at various points throughout the 1970s and 1980s. The official broadcasting line is that they won some battles and lost others; key to this folklore is a 1971 programme about which the BBC said they stood up to Tory assault and broadcast the programme anyway. But the folklore misses the point. Whether there was success or failure, each skirmish has led to increased caution, making it more difficult to make the next programme which may lead to confrontation with the state.

This leads to distorted coverage. For example, there are very few interviews with anybody who claims to speak on behalf of the IRA, INLA, etc. The last one was in 1979; before that, throughout the 1970s, there were only six each for ITN and the BBC. This extends to a lack of coverage of what Sinn Féin has to say. John Conway, former Head of BBC News in Northern Ireland, said, "We use sparingly the opportunity we have to interview Sinn Féin members and we never forget their links to violence."

In fact this was one of the arguments that the NUJ in Northern Ireland used in opposition to the broadcasting ban – the fact that they had not interviewed many republicans before the ban. Richard Francis, former BBC Controller in Northern Ireland, summed up the official attitude of the BBC when he said, "We do not deal impartially with those who step outside the bounds of the law and decent social behaviour. Not only do they get very much less coverage than those who pursue their aims legitimately, but the very manner and tone that our reporters have dubbed makes our moral position quite plain."

Finally, there is more leeway in the British legislation, in the British ban, than there is with RTE. Interestingly, that scope was underlined by the Home Office itself. The BBC fell over itself to be the most inflexible in interpreting the ban while Channel 4 pointed out initially that it also applied to works of fiction including feature films. The Home Office, however, claimed that "genuine works of fiction were not covered by the ban" and that "a member of an organisation can't be held to represent that organisation in all his (sic) daily activities". Unfortunately broadcasters have not used that scope, with the exception of Mary Holland, who interviewed Gerry Adams on Channel 4's

Dispatches; during that programme, Adams's words were spoken by Stephen Rea. Because it was so electronically synchronised that the join was unseen, it showed the ridiculousness of the ban in ways that Wesley Boyd's earlier statement does not.

To sum up. First, this may not be classic totalitarian censorship, but it is still censorship, and it works. It is a peculiarly democratic form of censorship. Second, Northern Ireland is central to this discussion. Despite all the run-ins that the British government had with broadcasters over the Belgrano, over *Spycatcher,* over Libya, over Zircon, at the core of most of these cases and the use of most of these laws is the question of Ireland. And third, censorship is derived from and enhances a censorship culture, especially in Ireland. It is not just that bans are extended beyond where they were intended to go. It is the fact that individuals and whole classes, whole communities of people are demonised and dis-enfranchised. The question of *The Street*, Gerry Adams's short stories, has been mentioned. In relation to RTE's refusal to advertise the book, it has been said:

> By depicting him solely as a beast, RTE is denying him his humanity and contributing to a climate of opinion whereby his murder will be welcomed.

That quote is not from *An Phoblacht*, but was written by Nick Garbutt, editor of the *Irish News*.

The measure of democracy is how society handles the extremes, not the every-day. How it encourages citizenship and a sense of belonging to minorities and those in the margins. In this sense, despite the sterling efforts of people like Roger Bolton, Ian Studdert and Mary Holland, democracy has been very badly served by the states in these islands and their respective broadcasting organisations.

DEMOCRACY AND FREEDOM OF INFORMATION

Frances D'Souza

ARTICLE 19 IS an international organisation concerned with promoting and campaigning for freedom of expression. Based in London, its brief is world-wide, helping to create a climate of freedom of expression, of non-secrecy, which we believe is a fundamental right. In the absence of freedom of expression other abuses of human rights, including killing people, can occur with impunity. Indeed, when a state of emergency is declared, the first thing a military government does is to collar the press and shut down or take control of broadcasting. Governments know that information is extremely powerful and it is very much in their interests to control it. Article 19 believes that unless there is freedom of information, of expression, of the press and of reporting, it is almost inevitable that the power of government will over-reach itself and abuses will occur.

These abuses are more dramatic and awful in some rather than other parts of the world. In Turkey today, journalists are being killed at an alarming rate. This seems to be a convenient form of censorship, particularly when there is failure to set up any kind of official murder inquiry. In Burma, there is almost a total clampdown on any kind of information. Likewise, concern has been expressed about many African and Middle Eastern countries. The list could go on and on.

Many of the ambassadors, chargés d'affaires or their secretaries at these missions and embassies ask why organisations such as Article 19 worry about their country rather than their own. This is a valid question. It is instructive for us to be concerned about the way in which democracy is eroded, and to question what is meant by democracy and how to uphold it. Therefore, how press laws or laws affecting the press, and their application in different western

European and North American democracies, has formed part of a wide-ranging comparative study. Eleven countries have been included in the study, the purpose of which is twofold.

First, many emerging democracies in eastern and central Europe and in Africa have begun to draft press laws. They have experienced, however, great difficulty in drafting appropriate legislation. An American lawyer suggested that he did not know what the problem was. "Why don't we just fax them our Constitution?" While this view was sincerely expressed, and indeed the US Constitution and First Amendment rights are certainly models, it is not a question of simply faxing models. Rather, it is a question of examining what works and what does not, as a guide, as an aid, to these drafting committees which are concerned with getting it right. Second, press self-regulation, something which has been promoted in the UK, has worked in some countries. It is important to understand better how it has worked and why.

The eleven countries under examination were: Australia, Austria, Canada, France, Germany, the Netherlands, Norway, Spain, Sweden, the UK and the USA. These countries were selected partly because of the expertise available to write detailed accounts, but also because these countries represent interesting aspects of the way in which the press is regulated. Twenty-two different characteristics affecting the press were compared, including constitutional provisions, other legal provisions or mechanisms, regulation of ownership, registration requirements, press self-regulation, prior restraint, right of reply, right of journalists to protect their sources, blasphemy and obscenity, restrictions on advertising, etc.

The cross-country study has been quite revealing. The country with the worst record of protecting the press is the UK, according to nine characteristics, *inter alia* constitutional and legal protections, self-regulation such as press councils, protection of journalists' sources, and privacy laws. In many of the countries under study, notably France, the press is restricted from reporting even on public figures. In other cases, notably the USA, there are no laws of privacy. Instead, there is a useful and clear distinction between a public person and a private individual, an important aspect of the question of privacy. However, in those countries with restrictions on the freedom of the press to report, there was enabling legislation which allowed access to information, such as a freedom of information act or other suitable legislation. The only country of the eleven which had restricted laws on the press, no positive formulations of the right to report and no legislation to allow access to information was the UK. Thus the UK, a traditional democracy, actually has only negative legislation about the press.

This is an extremely dangerous situation. To introduce legislation which would, in any way, restrict the reporting of the press, unless other legislation or constitutional provisions uphold freedom of expression – of which freedom of the press and access to information are crucial components – is dangerous. Once such a law is on the statute books, even in democracies, there is inevitably a tendency for the government to use that law in its own defence. Indeed, some people argue that there is no such thing as a good law *vis-à-vis* the press, and that may well be right. In countries which do not have strong protections for freedom of expression it is particularly dangerous because of the way in which authorities can use such laws against the less powerful.

The only other country in this study which has no constitutional or legal protection of the press is Australia which, on the whole, has inherited the traditional English view that freedom of speech is best protected by Common Law. Australia takes on a Commonwealth hue. Canada, also a Commonwealth country, however, has constitutional protection in the Bill of Rights and Civil Code, as do all the other countries studied. Even Spain, which would not be viewed as one of the most liberal democracies in Europe by virtue of tradition and recent history, does have constitutional protections and self-regulation.

Another important comparison was the degree to which these different countries incorporated international treaties – the International Covenant on Civil and Political Rights and the European Convention on Human Rights – which strongly uphold freedom of expression. The degree to which countries have incorporated these treaties into their domestic law essentially means that they can be used as a defence in a national court. The majority of countries incorporated these international treaties into their domestic law, except the UK and Australia.

Finally, there is a tendency in all the countries studied to allow a statutory right of reply. In some of the Scandinavian countries, notably Sweden, there is an obligation which newspapers and their editors accept to publish a right of reply or a correction. There is also a provision whereby newspapers can be fined substantial fines up to $4,000 if they get things wrong and it is considered abusive to the individual concerned. The UK does not have a statutory right of reply. The Press Council has few sanctions or teeth by which it can enforce or persuade newspapers that there is a line between protecting individual privacy and reporting on the life and work of public figures, notably the government.

This is a very short summary. The main point is that one cannot assume that the democratic practices of free and fair elections at reasonable regular periods is equal to a functioning democracy. The message of Article 19 is that democracy is an incredibly fragile process that requires constant vigilance. One of the best barometers of the extent to which human rights are respected in a society is the degree to which the press is free. If a free press is lost, then democracy is lost. There is a very great danger of that in the UK.

Dr Anthony Clare

BEFORE I ADDRESS the issue of reproductive rights, it is worth making a point or two about issues of access to information within medical practice, particularly a patient's access to his or her own records. In its own way, this has operated as a formal censorship until relatively recently. It is like so much censorship; it emerges from, not always malevolent, but often benevolent intentions. The history of medical practice up to the latter part of the twentieth century is the history of benevolence.

Prior to the specialisation of medicine and the scientific, technological revolution within medicine, the relationship between a doctor and a patient was a personal one. It was often an important relationship but a personal one nonetheless; the laying-on-of-hands, as Lewis Thomas has called it, rather than the reading of signals from machines. But in the development of scientific medicine, the detachment of patient from doctor has become perceptible. Information has become complicated. It has become technological. It has become expressed in a complex professional jargon, and in the 100 years or so since, the patient's relationship with the doctor has subtly and, indeed, not so subtly changed.

At the latter end of this century, a realisation developed that the patient's relationship with the doctor had become profoundly skewed. That the doctor, for good or ill, possessed power and information in such a way that the control by a patient of his or her own disease had been all but eliminated. Diseases and disorders became not what they are in truth, of the individual who suffers from them, but a rarefied object of which the doctor is expert, the doctor knows best and the doctor communicates in such a way as to invalidate the patient's own experience.

This is the basis on which the move for patient disclosure and access to medical records has operated. Many doctors have felt threatened by such a development but, in truth, if proper safeguards are developed, it does appear – as so often is the case with censorship – that the practice of medicine is profoundly improved. A patient's access to his or her records leads to a higher quality of record. It leads to the correction of mistakes. It leads to the correction of perception. It leads to greater care on the part of doctors in terms of what and the way they write, such that one might indeed be able on occasion to read it. And finally, there is very good evidence that it leads to a far greater degree of compliance on the part of patients with what their doctors actually recommend. All these benefits accrue from improving access to case records.

There is a problem in two areas: one is child care and the other mental health. Often information in relation to something like child sexual abuse, for example, is given by individuals to doctors on the assumption that the source of the information will be anonymous. One would not be able to proceed where information is provided without such guarantees. The person giving it often lives in close proximity to the patient and might find their relationship and, indeed, their safety threatened. The spouse, for example, of a potentially violent or alcoholic patient, or seriously psychotic patient, providing doctors with information of an important kind, would nonetheless be rendered vulnerable should that information or its source be made known to the individual patient. But these kinds of exceptions cannot be used to justify a blanket benevolence, a doctor-knows-best approach. Other reservations are that patients would not want to know certain aspects of their disease. Patients prefer not to know. All of these can be met. Indeed, a freedom of disclosure process does not mean that every patient demands access to their notes. Human nature being what it is, in those countries where access is mandatory, only a small minority of patients actually ask to see their files.

There are other censorship issues in medicine but this is an important moment for the issue of abortion or reproductive rights. With the formation of a new government, the referenda behind us and a legislation process ahead of us, it falls to me to remind you that the struggle over the reproductive rights of women in this country has only just begun. Indeed, there were things about the three referenda amendments that politics suggested were not said before the actual referenda but should be said now.

The whole notion of holding a referendum on women's access to information is such a profound disgrace for a nation such as this, with a constitution such as ours, that I, as a man, as a doctor, as a father and as a husband, feel almost moved to apologise to Irish women on behalf of what has primarily been a male-dominated, male-driven, male disgrace. Second, how relieved I was that the rest of the world's eyes were not focused on us, as some paranoid individuals appeared to believe, but were focused on many other more important things such as the trials and tribulations of our next-door neighbours. The world did not actually take to their hearts the notion that Ireland was seriously thinking of putting into its most revered document, a constitution, some kind of restriction on the right of women to move freely, not only in Ireland or indeed in Europe, but throughout the world. This notion seems absolutely unbelievable in retrospect but it happened, and the Irish people to their undying credit threw it out.

But the third issue is with us still. It is the substantive issue of abortion, and with it or surrounding it is a penumbra of issues such as the right of women to amniocentesis, tubal ligation, female and male sterilisation, and the provision of condoms. Our evasion of sexual education of an appropriate kind in our secondary schools means that this new government – whose ears must be ringing with the number of things all sorts of people are saying to them – must sit down and take a serious approach, properly informed, to the whole issue of rights in the reproductive area. These rights go beyond abortion to include the whole issue of a woman's right to understand and to control the nature of her procreative ability and, of course, men's right too.

The time for equivocation in relation to abortion is over. But the substantive issue of abortion was so brilliantly constructed that unless one stood like a tallyman as the votes fell out of the box, it was difficult to say whether the people who said "No", said "Yes, Yes" on the other two amendments or whether the people who said "No" said "No, No" on the other two amendments. It was impossible to decide whether people said "No" on the substantive issue because they were against abortion in all shapes or forms, or "No" because they would indeed abort anything that moved. I did stand for half an hour, and it seemed to me that the citizens in Palmerstown, west Dublin, voted about fifty-fifty.

That was a brilliant contribution from the last government. A piece of communication illustrating an adage that communication is not an ideal in itself because there are ways of communicating which leave the person who is communicated with no wiser than they were before they were communicated with in the first place. Now the Dáil and Senate will have to sit down and legislate on the substantive issue. Is there going to be a right of an Irish woman – pregnant as a result of rape or incest, or carrying an infant seriously at risk of foetal deformity, or profoundly suicidal in the case of carrying a pregnancy for those or other reasons – to have an abortion or not?

I for one am absolutely tired of people prevaricating on the issue of abortion. It is a very difficult decision. I find abortion or the practice of abortion difficult to acknowledge, but it is a fact. It is a right. It is one of the tests of us as a people in terms of coping with freedom and responsibility. Are we an adult people? Are we free to be given our rights? Are we free to make decisions and act on those decisions? Are we free to live in a society that recognises itself as a pluralist society in which, like it or not, we should face up to the fact that church of any kind and state are separate? Are we the kind of society which is prepared to tolerate that some people will take decisions which other people do not like? There is no question of making divorce, abortion or homosexuality mandatory.

In the midst of all these issues, Ireland is becoming an exciting place to live. One senses being on the edge of a moment when the Irish people, on a whole variety of issues, are not only going to be asked to say what they believe in terms of freedom and responsibilities, but they are going to be asked in a way that is comprehensible. In my view, we are going to have to answer in ways that are comprehensible, and we will have to live with that.

Aidan White

THE INTERNATIONAL FEDERATION of Journalists (IFJ) is a world-wide organisation of journalists and trade unionists which represents more than 300,000 journalists with member organisations in 70 countries. The aim of the IFJ is to bring together journalists around the world and, in the spirit of solidarity, to identify the issues where journalists and the media are under pressure and to try to co-ordinate responses to those problems.

This debate on secrecy and censorship is indeed timely. What is going on in Ireland is extremely important. But there is also change taking place in many parts of the world, particularly in Europe, Asia, Africa and Latin America. There is a great sense of debate and discussion in which the question of the flow of information has become ever more important as an international as well as a national issue. This is not an issue about the British Royal Family, but about the quality of democracy and the way society is developing.

Everywhere, in every part of the world, journalists are at the centre of this discussion and debate. Thus it is not surprising to find journalists under pressure, and paying a terrible price to enable this discussion. In 1992, in the region of 60 journalists were killed in the exercise of journalism. They were either shot by gangsters, caught in cross-fire conflict or were in the wrong place at the wrong time, but they were trying to do a job. The horrifying fact for complacent European democracies is that the most dangerous part of the world for journalists, in the last two years, has been in Europe and the Mediterranean area. There is no getting away from the fact that journalists who get too close to the story, who get too close to revealing the truth about what is going on in society, put themselves at risk. Whatever we do, we must recognise that fact and try to address it as a major problem.

In addition to the issue of violence against journalists, there are fundamental changes taking place in the economic and social life of the media which are causing enormous problems. The global media organisation and global restructuring of the media economy have brought with them enormous problems in terms of the cultural role of the media. The new and volatile business atmosphere in which journalists have to work is putting even greater pressure upon journalists professionally. The pressure to get the story and beat the opposition sees journalist working against journalist. Being motivated by the need to sell an extra copy, to get a higher rating, to satisfy the needs of the boss whose demands are essentially economic imperatives of profit and are not the professional and cultural imperative of serving the needs of society, has caused major problems.

One need only look at the National Union of Journalists in Britain, which has effectively been outlawed as a collective organisation to represent journalists' interests. Hundreds of collective agreements have been stripped and set aside. The experience of Britain has sent a very worrying signal throughout Europe. Everyone has a Thatcher anecdote, and they worry about the same thing happening in their country. In Sweden an important part of the collective contract, a simple paragraph, says:

A journalist has the right to refuse an assignment, to refuse an instruction from an employer or the employer's representative, or a public official, if to so do, or to carry out that instruction, would compromise their profession or their ethics, according to their conscience.

That is a fundamental right – the right of journalists to say no, to defend their own ethics from the demands that are increasingly put on a media competing for advertising markets.

What are the IFJ's objectives to resolve these problems? Of course it is necessary that we should have laws. The most important is freedom of information. Two or three years ago, the IFJ produced a report about the deplorable situation and the problem of secrecy in Ireland, particularly Section 31. The IFJ would like to see all mechanisms of secrecy removed and a freedom of information law introduced at European level. Article 10 of the European Convention on Human Rights provides the basis for legal and cultural policy within Europe but that article was ignored when Brussels bureaucrats drew up a law recently for control of official information. It looks as though that draft law was put together by Whitehall bureaucrats from the Conservative government. Happily, because of a campaign waged by Article 19 and other freedom of expression organisations, that particular law has been withdrawn, but it may be re-written into something else. We have to demand a European dimension to freedom of information which is reflected in directives and in practice.

There also needs to be a proper legal basis for protection of sources. Journalists and media organisations are being fined, and in Australia people have been sent to prison because of their refusal to give sources of information. Confidentiality, for journalists, is a prime tool by which they operate. That is also a law the IFJ would demand. But most importantly, there needs to be a structure which empowers journalists to act professionally without undue influence, either from ideological or economic forces. France, Scandinavia and other countries recognise a clause of conscience – the right of editorial staff and journalists to refuse to be told what to do, to refuse to use a cheque book to buy a story or to invade someone's privacy if they think it is against their ethics.

The right of a journalist to say "no" has to be embodied in proper editorial statutes. That means journalists must be involved in the question of editors. Editors hold a very ambiguous role: they are employers, but also journalists and defenders of the public interest. Journalists should have a responsibility in their appointment. They should be involved in the definition of editorial policy and in the question of personnel policies. It is important to create a situation in which journalists work in an environment where the editorial area is open, ethical and accountable. That is the aim of the IFJ.

Patrick Smyth

A FEW DAYS ago, the 1932 state papers were published. The *Irish Independent* published a story from them which seemed particularly apt. Very briefly, it was the story of a Protestant missionary who went to Granard, Co. Longford, in 1932. He stayed in a local bed and breakfast place and received a parcel of books from his organisation. The landlady decided that she did not approve of the books and, instead of handing them over to her guest, took them down to the parish priest. The parish priest organised a group of vigilantes to come down to the house, beat him up and drive him out of town. That was Granard, 1932. In Tuam, 1992, Kathleen Meehan stood up in a church – some say she was a little emotional, whatever – and disrupted the service. She was taken out of the church by force and charged under the Ecclesiastical Courts Act of 1860 with "violent behaviour in a place of religious worship during the celebration of divine service which did disquiet the preacher". She received a sentence of two months for it; the case is on appeal.* This is one of the most appalling violations of people's rights in many years. What kind of a country is this that we feel so insecure? That we believe that our institutions are so weak that we need the full force of the law to be applied to an obstreperous lady in a church?

Salman Rushdie was absolutely right when he said that with censorship we are concerned with difficult cases, those that make us wince a bit; those with which we are not particularly happy to be associated. One can oppose abortion and still believe that women have a right to know. One can believe that Madonna's book is a silly piece of trivia but still believe it is foolish in the extreme to ban it. One can oppose the Provisional IRA and still believe Section 31 is wrong and foolish.

This conference has drawn all of these issues together under the banner of freedom of information in order to create a broader consensus. A campaign about freedom of information allows us to

*Kathleen Meehan was successful in her appeal against her conviction.

advance on all these fronts, to challenge archaic and disgraceful laws. For too long these issues have been ghettoised; people who picked up particular issues have been stigmatised. For too long, a paternalistic nanny state has told us that we must be protected from ourselves, has thought for us, has given us no credit for any maturity, has thought that if we know too much of the truth we might come to the wrong conclusions and that our faith in the status quo might be shaken.

Information is considered subversive. Rather, it is corruption in government and business, hypocrisy and cant, bureaucracy and self-serving golden circles which threaten our democracy – not information. If we put our faith in ordinary people, trust them to take decisions, give them the information to make those decisions, the streets of our cities are not going to run with blood. On the contrary, things are likely to work better. We are likely to expose corruption. We are likely to expose inefficiency. What will happen? A free flow of information is like oxygen to the body of politics. Without it the body atrophies and dies. With it, the body works efficiently. This conference is not about the freedom of the press. It is about the freedom of the citizen. It is about confidence in our people, in our maturity and in our democracy. Promises are not enough. The new government's promise to look at a freedom of information bill is not enough. We want a freedom of information bill; we demand a freedom of information bill. This conference has put freedom of information and censorship firmly at the centre of the political agenda in this country. We are saying to Albert Reynolds and his government, in the Taoiseach's own words: "Let in the Light".

An Appeal

WE, THE UNDERSIGNED, call for a public debate on secrecy, censorship and democracy in Ireland. We believe that a culture of secrecy pervades whole areas of our society – and betrays a lack of faith in the strength of our democracy.

Legislative reform and a radical change in the climate of official secrecy are required now. To help bring about such change, an informed public debate is needed to address:

The reform of the Official Secrets Act and the enactment of a freedom of information act containing a positive assertion of the right to information;

The outdated and restrictive defamation laws and the need to implement the Law Reform Commission's proposals;

The continuing use of censorship laws against publications, films and the arts;

Political censorship through the Offences Against the State Act and Section 31 of the Broadcasting Act, distorting the coverage of the Northern conflict

The need for public accountability in business and commerce; the need for full access to medical and reproductive information.

We support the convening of a public conference in January 1993 to lay the basis for a public debate on these issues.

Brian Anderson, Brendan Archbold, William Attley, Robert Ballagh, John Banville, Eileen Battersby, Dr Patricia Behan, Neil Belton, Dr Moosajee Bhamjee TD, Siobhan Bourke, Philip Boxburger, Brian Boyd, Roisín Boyd, Prof. Kevin Boyle, Maxine Brady, Ronan Brady, Declan Bree TD, John Breen, Joe Broderick, Bernard Browne, Harry Browne, Vincent Browne, Declan Burke-Kennedy, Don Buckley, Eric Byrne, Ray Byrne, Ann Cadwallader, Anne Cahill, Dick Cahill, Prof. Nicholas Canny, Mary Carolan, Father Denis Carroll, Joe Carroll, Dr Anthony Clare, Frank Clarke SC, David Collins, Patrick Comerford, Evelyn Conlon, Anne Connolly, Tom Cooney, Kevin Cooper, Dr Farrell Corcoran, Mary Corcoran, Dr Anthony Coughlan, Carol Coulter, Anastasia Crickley, Anne Crilley, Niall Crowley, Mary Cullen, Joe Culley, John Cunningham, John Daly, Renagh Dardis, Gerald Dawe, Prof. Seamus Deane, Deaglán de Bréadún, Simon Devilly, Donagh

Diamond, Siobhan Doherty, Jarlath Dolan, Lelia Doolan, James Downey, Roddy Doyle, Joe Duffy, Myles Dungan, Sean Dunne, Jim Eadie, Prof. Brian Farrell, Michael Farrell, Peter Feeney, Kieron Fitzgerald, Dr Ann Flynn, Mary Flynn, Phil Flynn, Michael Foley, Dr Tadgh Foley, John Foster, Brian Friel, Terry George, Des Geraghty MEP, Luke Gibbons, Michael Gill, Johnny Gogan, Nóirín Greene, Eithne Hand, Ellen Hazelkorn, Maurice Hearne, John Hedges, Tricia Hegarty, Micheal Heney, Dr Mary Henry, Kintilla Heussaff, Brian Higgins, Michael D. Higgins TD, Mary Holland, Dr John Horgan, Jean Horgan, Ruth Hosty, Declan Hughes, Janet Hughes, Tom Humphries, Dr Attracta Ingram, Tim Jenkins, Jennifer Johnston, Michael Johnston, Tony Jones, Barbara Jordan, Dr Richard Kearney, Justin Keating, Una Keating, John Kelly, Mary Kelly, Nuala Kelly, Paddy Kelly, Ronan Kelly, Vincent Kelly, Prof. Brendan Kennelly, Dr Colum Kenny, Colin Kerr, Colm Keena, Declan Kiberd, Sean Kilfeather, Peadar Kirby, Arthur Lappin, Christy Loftus, Angela Long, Mary Maher, Louis Marcus, Dr Sean Marlow, Proinsias MacAonghusa, Stephanie McBride, Tiernan MacBride, Eugene McCabe, Nell McCafferty, Eamonn McCann, Barry McCall, Jim McCullagh, Susan McKay, Frank McDonald, Micheál Mac Donnchada, Steve MacDonogh, Dr Margaret MacCurtain, Uinsionn Mac Dubhghaill, Marie McGonagle, Freda McGough, Finian McGrath, Alva MacSharry, John Masterson, Greg Maxwell, Niall Meehan, Matt Merrigan, Ed Moloney, Mary Morrissy, John Mulcahy, Eilís Mullan, Pat Murphy, Patsey Murphy, Ray Murphy, Kevin Myers, Conor Norton, Brendan O'Brien, Brendan O'Cathaoir, Ronan O'Donoghue, Liam O'Dowd, Nollaig Ó Gadhra, Sarah O'Hara, Fergus O'Hare, Gerry O'Hare, Rita O'Hare, Donal O'Kelly, Aileen O'Meara, Máirtín Ó Muilleóir, Antóin Ó Muircheartaigh, Emily O'Reilly, Noelle O'Reilly, Kevin O'Sullivan, Niamh O'Sullivan, Fintan O'Toole, Senator Joe O'Toole, Larry O'Toole, Lynn Parker, Robin Percival, Cathal Póirtéir, Paddy Prendiville, Norma Prendiville, Betty Purcell, Arthur Quinlan, David Rice, Michael Ritchie, Chris Robson, Kevin Rockett, Dr Bill Rolston, Eoin Ronayne, Kieran Rose, Senator Brendan Ryan, Dr Angela Savage, Dr Michael Scott, David Shanks, Ella Shanahan, Dr Helena Sheehan, Ronan Sheehan, Kathy Sheridan, Peter Sheridan, Dave Sholdice, Lorna Siggins, Ailbhe Smyth, Patrick Smyth, R. Smyth, Ann Speed, Roy Spence, Emmet Stagg TD, Sheila Sullivan,

Dan Sullivan, Jimmy Sommers, Noreen Thompson, John Tierney, Mike Tomlinson, Dr Brian Torode, Brian Trench, Julian Vignoles, John Walshe, Profesor Jim Ward, Ken Whelan, Alex White, Robin Wilson, Dr Moira Woods, Emer Woodfull, John Wyse Jackson.

Supporting organisations: National Union of Journalists, SIPTU, MSF, USI, Brandon Book Publishers, GLEN, Irish National Congress, Writers' Union, WERRC, ICCL, Article 19, Gyre and Gimble Theatre Company, Gill and Macmillan, Anvil Books.

Contributors

Robert Ballagh is an artist and founding president of the Association of Artists in Ireland.

Carl Bernstein is a journalist; he and Bob Woodward, as staff reporters of the *Washington Post*, successfully uncovered much of the story of the Watergate break-in and cover-up, which they described in *All the President's Men*.

Neil Belton is Editorial Director of Jonathan Cape.

Kevin Boyle is Professor of Law and Director of the Human Rights Centre at the University of Essex; he is a consultant to the National Newspapers of Ireland on media law.

Maxine Brady is a former president of the Union of Students in Ireland; she was successfully sued, with other student leaders and unions, by the Society for the Protection of Unborn Children for disseminating information about abortion.

Anthony Clare is Professor of Psychiatry in Trinity College, Dublin, Master of St Patrick's Hospital, and a broadcaster.

David Collins is an independent film producer and former film officer of the Arts Council.

Frances D'Souza is General Secretary of Article 19, the international campaign against censorship.

Jake Ecclestone is Deputy General Secretary of the National Union of Journalists and a former journalist on *The Times*.

Garret FitzGerald, a former Taoiseach, is an economist and columnist.

Luke Gibbons is a lecturer in Communications at Dublin City University.

Ellen Hazelkorn is a lecturer in Politics at the Dublin Institute of

Technology, and treasurer of "Let in the Light".

Mary Holland is a columnist with *The Irish Times* and *The Observer*.

Damien Kiberd, a former *Irish Press* business editor, is now editor of the *Sunday Business Post*.

Anthony Lewis is a columnist with the *New York Times*.

Patrick MacEntee is a Senior Counsel and a former chairman of the Bar Council of Ireland.

Steve MacDonogh is Editorial Director of Brandon.

Michael Mills is a former political correspondent of the *Irish Press* and now the Ombudsman.

Marie McGonagle is a lecturer in law at University College, Galway, a consultant to the National Newspapers of Ireland on media law, and a committee member of "Let in the Light".

Susan O'Keeffe is a journalist with Granada's *World in Action* who broke the Goodman story. She was ordered by the Beef Industry Tribunal to reveal her sources and refused.

Cathleen O'Neill is a worker with the women's community arts group KLEAR, based at the Kilbarrack Adult Education Centre.

Mary Raftery is a journalist and producer, predominantly for RTE. Her programme on the Gallagher scandal won a Jacobs award, and she is a former Woman Journalist of the Year.

Bill Rolston is a lecturer in Communications at the University of Ulster.

Salman Rushdie is the author of the Booker Prize-winning *Midnight's Children* and of *The Satanic Verses* which resulted in February 1989 in the issuing of a *fatwa*, or religious edict, by the late Ayatollah Khomeni sentencing him to death.

Patrick Smyth is the Foreign News Editor of the *Irish Times* and secretary of "Let in the Light".

John Tierney is National Officer, Ireland, of the union MSF.

Aidan White is the General Secretary of the International Federation of Journalists and a former *Guardian* journalist.

Alex White is Senior Producer of the Gay Byrne Show and a committee member of "Let in the Light".

Michael D. Higgins
With drawings by Mick Mulcahy
THE SEASON OF FIRE

An accomplished and fascinating second collection of poetry from
Michael D. Higgins, Minister for the Arts, Culture and the
Gaeltacht, illustrated with original drawings by Mick Mulcahy.
Following the remarkable success of his first collection, *The
Betrayal*, this new book shows a deepening of the intensity and a
development of the range of his poetry.

"There's an immediacy about Michael D. Higgins' poetry that I have
always found attractive.... Michael D. doesn't just write *about*
people; he excels at writing directly *to* them." *Brendan Kennelly*

"Higgins takes risks in both personal and poetic terms, and the
poems bear witness to the honesty of dangerous self-revelation.
They occasionally have a strangely sad sense of fun, especially
those dealing with the world of acedemic work... Yet fear of loss,
insecurity, uncertainty, perhaps envy, reveal their uncomfortable
faces too. " *Irish Reporter*

Gerry Adams
THE STREET AND OTHER STORIES

"The Street is not so much a fictional microcosm of Adams's
world; it is the world itself... a small world, but a rich one, and
lovingly recreated by Adams in small-scale, understated and domestic stories." *Times Literary Supplement*

"He brings a wry humour and a detailed observation to small
events. ...If there is a unifying strand, it is compassion for people
in difficult situations." *Sunday Times*

Also published by Brandon

Steve MacDonogh (ed) in association with Article 19
THE RUSHDIE LETTERS:
FREEDOM TO SPEAK, FREEDOM TO WRITE

This important book documents the international response of writers to the most extreme example of literary censorship in modern times. At the heart of it are letters to Rushdie, many of them moving and passionate, and Salman Rushdie's essay, "1,000 Days in a Balloon".

"A powerful and intensely moving collection of letters... a stirring indictment of censorship in contemporary life." *Booklist*

"Under ordinary circumstances, publication of letters from authors such as Günter Grass, Nadine Gordimer, Norman Mailer, and Margaret Atwood would be a significant literary event. But *The Rushdie Letters*, which includes two letters from the condemned author, reaches beyond the world of literature, offering an emotional and inspiring reflection on the personal and global issues at stake in the 'Rushdie Affair'." *Boston Phoenix*